What happened the last time you ran for a bus? Have twenty cigarettes a day become thirty? Does your total exercise consist of reaching for the phone or taking the cover off your typewriter? Vital questions.

Over 30,000 people in Britain will die prematurely during the next year of heart disease. Many will be overweight, heavy smokers, and sedentary.

Fit for Life tells you how you can reduce the risk of heart trouble, chronic bronchitis, obesity, arthritis and some stress diseases, without drastically altering the pattern of your life. And it can be fun!

Dr. H. Beric Wright is Medical Director of the Institute of Directors, and with Dr. G. Pincherle, British Heart Foundation Research Fellow at the Institute's Medical Centre, has carried out an extensive survey into stress and other causes of illness amongst men and women executives.

Al Murray, M.S.R.G., is Britain's National and Olympic Coach for weightlifting and has trained many top athletes. A qualified remedial gymnast, he is an expert in the field of physical fitness.

Fit for Life

Health and heart disease

H. Beric Wright, M.B., F.R.C.S.
Director
G. Pincherle, M.B., Ch.B., M.R.C.P.
Deputy Director (Research)
Institute of Directors' Medical Centre, London

Al Murray, M.S.R.G.
British National and Olympic Coach
Director
City Gymnasium, London

 Evans Brothers Limited London

Published by Evans Brothers Limited
Montague House, Russell Square,
London, WC1
© H. Beric Wright, G. Pincherle, Al Murray
and ABC Television Limited, 1968
First published 1968

Based on ABC Television series 'Fit for Life'

Set in 10 on 12 Baskerville and printed in
Great Britain by Cox and Wyman Ltd., London,
Fakenham and Reading.
CSD 237   35074   2
PB 237   35075   0   PR 4596

Contents

List of Figures

List of Tables

The publishers acknowledge the help of
George Grose Limited, for kindly supplying references
for physical fitness equipment.

Illustrations by Victor Reinganum

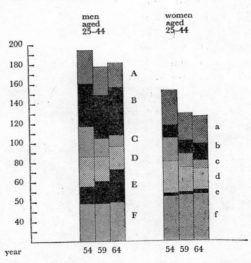

(Aa) other causes. (Bb) all violent causes. (Cc) respiratory disease including all forms of tuberculosis (Dd) other cardiovascular disease including cerebro-vascular disease. (Ee) arteriosclerotic disease. (Ff) malignant disease.

Fig. 1(a)

1 How healthy are we?

Britain has always taken pride in its social and welfare services which started with the Poor Law during the industrial revolution (1834), were developed by Lloyd George after the 1914–18 war, who introduced the panel system of medical insurance and treatment, and finally reached maturity with the Labour government 'welfare state' in 1948. This was based on the Beveridge Report, published just before the end of the war and provided an outline plan for more or less unified Health and Social Security services which were free at the point of consumption. Foreigners tend to think that we have free medicine in this country, but in fact the service costs many millions of pounds annually and is paid for by workers' and employers' contributions and out of direct taxation. In fact 81 per cent is paid for by the exchequer.

Under this system citizens are entitled to 'free' general practitioner, hospital and rehabilitation services, including drugs and various aids for disability. Britain pioneered this approach to medical welfare, but in fact we now spend less per capita than do many European countries. But what benefit do we, as a nation, obtain from all this expenditure? One would be tempted to think, superficially at any rate, that with this extensive provision for sickness and emergency, our health should be better now than it ever has been.

But is it? The short and statistical answer is that it does not really seem to be better. It is true that diseases of poverty and malnutrition have largely been abolished, that antibiotics control

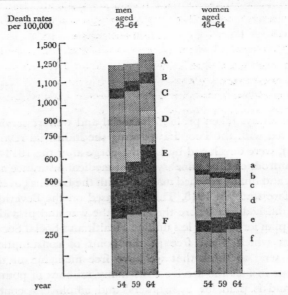

Death rates per 100,000

men aged 45–64

women aged 45–64

(Aa) other causes (Bb) all violent causes. (Cc) respiratory disease including all forms of tuberculosis (Dd) other cardiovascular disease including cerebro-vascular disease. (Ee) arteriosclerotic disease. (Ff) malignant disease.

FIG. 1(b)

acute infective diseases and that mass radiography and streptomycin have made Tuberculosis a relatively uncommon condition.

If, however, one looks at Fig. 1 which shows the main causes of death for men and women over the past 10 years, it is clear that the overall death rate for men in either of the three age groups has not fallen appreciably over the period: the rate for women has gone down, but only marginally. But more important than the total death rate is the proportion of deaths caused by individual diseases or conditions.

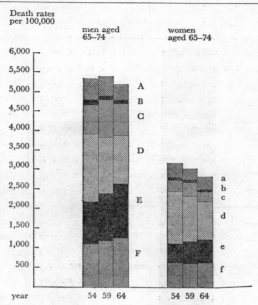

(Aa) other causes. (Bb) all violent causes. (Cc) respiratory disease including all forms of tuberculosis. (Dd) other cardiovascular disease including cerebro-vascular disease. (Ee) arteriosclerotic heart disease. (Ff) malignant disease.

FIG. 1(c)

FIG. 1 (a)(b)(c). The main causes of death: the vertical scale in these charts shows the death rate per 100,000 in each age group. For men, this rises from 200 in the 24–44 to over 5,000 in the oldest group. The corresponding death rates for women are appreciably lower.
Within each group various shaded areas indicate the individual causes of death. Source: Registrar General.

A further look at Fig. 1 reveals some fascinating facts. Firstly that in younger men accidents and violence – road accidents, industrial and domestic accidents – are the biggest single cause of death. Secondly, that even at this relatively young age,

13

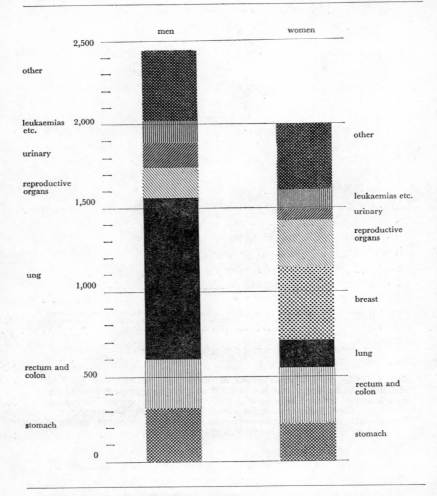

Fig. 2. Death rates from various types of cancer, for men and women of all ages in 1965, per 100,000 of the population. Source: Registrar General.

cardiovascular disease (coronary thrombosis, high blood pressure and strokes) is beginning to take its toll.

Looking at the next age group, 45–64 – which embraces men in their prime of life – it is seen that not only is this the biggest single cause of death, but that its incidence is increasing rather than diminishing. The last and older age group shows much the same thing, but it is less important because individuals in this group are reaching the age when they must die of something and the cause is relatively unimportant.

Thirdly and most interesting of all, we can see from the figures that 'rate for age' women have a lower death rate than men and that in the two older groups it is in fact about half that of men; this difference being largely due to women not getting cardiovascular disease and chronic bronchitis to anything like the same extent.

This difference in death rates presents a major point of medical interest for which there is no easy explanation. It explains why there are so many widows in the community and why rich Americans tend to be widows. It suggests too that women appear tougher and fitter than men and also that when they are young they seem to be able to avoid violent death. Thus, if an individual wants to have the maximum chances of surviving, he ought to be a woman!

In all these age groups cancer plays a part and accounts for about a third of deaths, but when this is broken down into individual cancers (Fig. 2) it is seen that although remaining important, lung cancer for instance, kills far fewer people than heart disease.

If then death rates are altering little and cardiovascular disease is increasing, what about ordinary sickness and industrial absenteeism? Surely it might be thought, our splendid health service is keeping more people at work and reducing the incidence of the simpler and seldom fatal diseases.

Table 1 shows the number of days lost over the last few

TABLE 3

DAYS LOST BY THE INSURED POPULATION IN BRITAIN

Year	Total days lost in millions	Sickness benefits			Injury benefit		Total days lost insured women
		Psychiatric	Accidents	Other	Accidents	Prescribed disease	
1953–4	203·88	13·20	12·66	160·9	15·92	1·20	96·41
1957–8	218·14	15·77	13·26	173·66	14·67	0·78	91·93
1963–4	230·73	17·66	18·80	175·29	18·36	0·62	78·0
1965–6	256·02	18·17	21·36	195·61	20·21	0·67	79·70

Source: Ministry of Social Security.

years by insured people entitled to sickness benefit. Looking at these you will see that far from there being a reduction in sickness absence, it is in point of dismal fact tending to increase year by year. The average man loses 14 and the average woman loses 21 days per year. The table also shows some of the causes for this lost time. We also have figures which show that various professional groups, who are more highly motivated to work, lose much less time although they can 'go sick' when they want to.

This is not the time or the place to discuss the reasons for this situation in any detail, except to make two points. First, that medically, chronic bronchitis – known abroad as English Disease – and rheumatism are a major cause of illness. Chronic bronchitis is due to two things, the cold damp climate and inhaling cigarettes.

We worry about air pollution and have controlled smog in many parts of the country, but inhaling cigarette smoke is concentrated air pollution which literally knocks the lining off the lungs.

Second, that we all know from our own experience that much of this sickness is not real, to the extent that there are many people who could go to work either if they really wanted to, if they absolutely had to, or if it was worth their while to do so. To a degree part of Britain's current national malaise is due to a disinclination or a lack of real motivation to work. This can be regarded as mental ill health and is a reflection of the growing toll of mental disease and psychiatric breakdown. It is not generally realized that 45 per cent of the hospital beds in Britain are for mental disease.

If this absenteeism could be reduced by, say, one-third, all our problems of productivity might be solved.

Taking these two sets of figures together it can, we think, be said fairly, that the people of Britain are not particularly healthy and that anything that can reasonably be done to deal with this situation is likely to be of personal and national benefit.

This book has two purposes, firstly to point out what some of the health snags are and secondly, to suggest ways in which individuals can get the best out of life – but yet enjoy what they do and lead exciting and useful lives.

2 What is Health?

Theoretically and for many years doctors have been brought up to believe that prevention is better than cure. But in practice they are trained in hospitals which exist to treat the sick and this is what they, of necessity, spend their lives doing. Britain has a National Health Service, but heaven knows how it ever got this name because none of it is preventive and all its agencies, general and special hospitals and family doctors, spend their whole time treating illness or disease. It should in fact have been called the National Sickness Service. Such preventive work as is done, is the responsibility of the local authority and public health services.

This state of affairs developed because priorities have to be kept in perspective and there was, and indeed still is, a vast amount of disease which must be dealt with. The figures already quoted support this situation, but if we are ever to reduce the load on the hospitals and the queues in the surgeries, disease has to be dealt with before it produces enough damage to bring the sufferers for treatment. We think that an exciting new era of preventive medicine is starting and that it will be based on promoting health rather than treating disease.

The present state of our thinking and practice has for these reasons led us to think of health in the rather negative terms of the mere absence of disease. If one is not obviously ill one must be reasonably well.

This may be broadly and pedantically true, but it is not a good enough definition of health because we are increasingly finding that health is a positive entity related to the individuals well-being and *joie de vivre*. Because all research and study has been aimed at sick people we know little about the healthy, we cannot yet measure health except in 'absence of disease terms' and we find it difficult to define.

The World Health Authority in the post-war period of euphoria and great expectations, when everyone was engaged in writing blue prints for their slice of Utopia, got to work on preventive medicine. They defined health as 'a state of physical, mental and social well-being'.

This is an interesting and important definition because it relates the healthy man to his environment and it suggests that his mental and social well-being may be related to his physical state. The growth of what is called psychosomatic medicine – the effect of the mind on the body – has strengthened belief in the importance of this concept (psyche applies to the mind and soma the body). Certain diseases or conditions of disease are now generally believed to arise directly from stress or conflict and there are those who believe that virtually all illness is basically psychosomatic in origin.

We have already implied that the relationship between the individual and his environment – how he lives and spends his time – plays a major part in influencing his coronary proneness. We have also made the point that problems of mental health are important in the overall sickness rate. For these and other reasons which will later become apparent, it is necessary for the reader to have some understanding of the nature of stress and its relation to health.

Stress is a word which has been borrowed by medicine and biology, from engineering and physics. In these sciences it means an ability to withstand strain and is a finite and measurable quality. Thus an engineer building a bridge or the jib of a crane is able to calculate the load it can carry, and knows that if this load is exceeded the structure will collapse or bend. Indeed, structural mechanics have now taken this further and found that by pre-stressing certain materials like concrete, they can increase its strength.

Biologically all living things are in a state of constant battle with their environment. Plants have to obtain nutrition from the soil and stand up to or adapt to the climate. Similarly animals, birds, fishes and insects are, in much the same way, engaged in a constant battle against the world – or rather the small part of it in which they live. The mere fact of existing gives them a constant challenge which has to be overcome if they are to survive. Again in biological terms there has to be a considerable measure of adaptation to the environment if life is to be successful. Darwin described this as the survival of the fittest and postulated that over the millennia it was the basis of evolution.

In this respect man is no different from other forms of life, although he does have certain advantages – but as we shall see in Chapter 7 his very success is becoming a difficulty. What man has done is to learn to create his own artificial environment, he is kept warm, clothed, sheltered, fed and supplied with electricity and running water. But he still has to compete with his fellow humans – and on the whole he is, so far at any rate, not proving very clever at this.

Coming back to biology, challenge from the environment is essential to life. For man it is the overcoming of this challenge – in large ways and small ways – that gives tone and satisfaction to existence. On this basis one can say that each individual is in a constant relationship with the environment round him. Individuals differ in their skills and abilities and environments also differ. We have just said the physical environment dominates the life of plants and animals, for most men it is relatively unimportant. What is important is the environment of human and inter-personal relations. This is intensely complicated and made up of work groups, family groups, social groups – all of which make up the community: which has then to similarly relate to other local, national and international communities.

All these factors bring subtle pressures to bear on the individual and determine his reaction to situations. It is, in fact, this psychosocial environment which is increasingly important in today's man-made world.

The point to grasp at this stage in our argument is that the individual is constantly battling with his physical and psychosocial environment and he needs at least to break even in the struggle if he is to survive. This means that he must be in a reasonable state of equilibrium and thus his interaction can be regarded as an equation – a personality environment equation, which must be kept more or less stable or balanced.

If stability or balance is required for survival – or health – what happens when he is faced with defeat? It is in fact the possibility of defeat which sets in chain all the defence mechanisms which the psychosomatists believe make for the difference between health and disease – hence its relevance to our present theme.

If an animal is cornered, either by an enemy or by an external situation – floods, fires, water or food shortage, etc., it will do one of two things – fight or flight. Turn round and face the odds, or run away. Similarly, if an individual is metaphorically cornered by an uncongenial situation, he will either lash out at the environment often quite irrationally, perhaps by losing his temper, or he will retreat into himself and become quiet and introspective. In practice extroverts tend to lash out and introverts to 'curl up'.

This is, of course, an over-simplification of the grosser forms of what must be a complicated situation. But clearly there must be a basic biological defence mechanism against uncongenial situations – and indeed there is. The Victorians, particularly the ladies, were very good at getting 'the vapours', headaches and bilious attacks, when asked to do something they did not want to do. What we are postulating is that if an individual is unable to deal with his environment he develops symptoms which cause him to feel pain, be unable to function or be diseased. In fact illness seen in this light is a process of opting out of the environment. The personality environment equation gets out of balance, symptoms supervene and there is an escape into illness. On this basis ill health is a defence mechanism for inability to deal with life. And on this basis it is possible to see why life today with all its seeming advantages in practice causes more ill health than ever before.

But you, the reader, must by now be saying, all this is much too over-simplified and mechanistic – in any case, I get pain when I am ill, or I have a fever, or a tummy upset or jaundice or spots – and so on. True you do, and of course you will continue so to do. But what no one has yet investigated, and this comes back to what we said earlier about doctors being disease orientated, is why in an epidemic, for instance, relatively few people get ill and the rest survive. There is more to be learnt from the survivors – those who don't get typhoid, polio or flu, etc. – than from those who do.

We should qualify what we have said about disease being a process of 'opting' out and be clear that this process takes place at a subconscious level. The individual is quite unaware of what is happening. It is his psyche reacting automatically on his soma, that causes his symptoms. The reaction is, of course, complicated and determined not only by his genetic inheritance, but also by his upbringing which conditions his basic reaction to life. It was Freud's great contribution to point out that not only was much of behaviour determined by subconscious reactions, but that these were themselves determined or conditioned by the individual's early experiences in his relation with his environment, particularly his parents.

Space does not permit us to go further into this theme, but we started off by saying that health is a state of physical, mental and social well-being. We can, as a result of our further considerations, put this slightly differently and say that symptoms

23

of ill health are likely to arise if an individual is unable to stand up to the pressures of his immediate environment. That is, when his personality environment equation becomes unbalanced. It means that the healthy person is one who deals with the challenge that confronts him – and gets satisfaction out of it and that the ill person has probably failed.

This is a new concept of health with which not all doctors will agree, and it must be realized that it has been expressed in over-simplified terms. Whether or not it can really be extended for all types of illness only the future will tell. But if there is anything in it at all, it means that the healthy man is the one who succeeds in meeting his challenge or equating his aspirations and his attributes. To do this he must have enough insight to understand what stress is all about and also enough sense to realize what his limitations are so that he is not over-challenged. Various things can help him to do this and some of the pitfalls of cardiovascular disease, bronchitis and obesity can also be avoided. Most of this book will be devoted to discussing these, but a little more is said about living with stress in Chapter 11.

A healthy person is nearly always a happy, fulfilled person who knows where he wants to go and chooses the right place and the best route. If his social and mental well-being is good, his physical self is likely to stand up well to the demands he makes on it – provided the temptations of affluent over-indulgence and physical idleness are largely avoided.

Just as mind and body cannot be separated, so does the (broadly defined) health of the individual depend on the way in which he regulates his life to cope with the problems it sets him. As we shall hope to show, it is possible to load the 'health dice' in one's favour, by learning to live sensibly, equally, if one is overweight, physically idle, stressed and a cigarette addict, one is increasing the odds against oneself.

3 Your heart and what it does

Since classical times the heart has been regarded as the seat of the emotions and emotional conditions – fear, elation and so on have been known to influence the heart-beat.

Although all this is broadly true, the heart is a muscular pump which drives the blood continuously round the body. If the heart stops death supervenes, not just because of heart failure, but because the brain and other vital organs have an inadequate blood supply to keep them functioning. In this respect the blood and all that it contains is more vital than the heart – except that it has to be kept moving.

The blood consists of solid cells suspended in a complicated liquid called the plasma. The red cells carry oxygen to the tissues and help bring back carbon dioxide which is also carried in the plasma. Oxygen is required for energy production and the carbon dioxide is produced as a bi-product of its use. To provide oxygen and get rid of carbon dioxide the blood is pumped round the lungs where it is exposed to air through very thin spongy membranes.

Blood also has a wide range of other functions such as combating infection and providing food and other sorts of energy, these functions are outside our present scope.

As readers will know from their first aid and biology training, venous blood flows back to the right side of the heart through large veins. It collects in the right atrium or auricle which when full contracts and passes the blood into the right ventricle. As the atrium contracts to squeeze the blood on, pressure rises and closes simple flap valves over the openings of the large veins.

Without these the blood would obviously go straight back into the veins. The ventricle being empty is under less pressure and is filled by the contracting auricle, which, of course, empties.

When it is in turn full the ventricle contracts and squeezes out its contents, the rise in pressure closing another valve between auricle and ventricle. Blood from the right ventricle goes to the lungs where it gets oxygenated and returns to the left side of the heart as arterial blood.

Here it goes through a similar process and is pumped out by the ventricle into the arterial system and round the body.

The heart is thus two separate pumping systems, one for the lungs – the pulmonary – and the other for the body – the systemic circulations. The two sides are divided by a partition or septum which keeps venous and arterial blood separate. If there

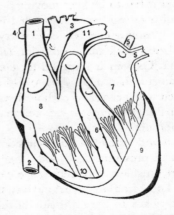

Fig. 3. Diagrammatic section through the heart to show the main chambers and vessels. 1. Superior vena cava. 2. Inferior vena cava. 3. Aorta. 4. Branches of right pulmonary veins. 5. Pulmonary artery. 6. Interventricular septum. 7. Left auricle. 8. Right auricle. 9. Left ventricle. 10. Right ventricle. 11. Left branch of pulmonary artery.

should be a hole in this septum two things will happen, first the heart will not function properly because the blood will go in the wrong direction; second, and more important, the venous and arterial blood gets mixed. This is the basis of 'holes in the heart' and explains why the babies which have them are blue – the so-called blue or venous baby (Fig. 3).

The heart functions as a whole, both auricles contracting together, followed by both ventricles. Obviously in a closed system like this, each of the four chambers must be the same size, but if the work load is different the power required will vary. Thus the atria or upper chambers have thin walls as they only have to collect blood from the veins and push it into the ventricles. Similarly the right ventricle only has to push blood round the lungs which is less work than has to be done by the left ventricle in pushing the blood right round the body. Thus the left ventricle is thicker and more muscular than the right.

The heart is controlled and co-ordinated in a variety of ways too complicated to go into, but clearly there have to be two mechanisms, one to keep the heart itself beating effectively so that the atria fill the ventricles before the latter contract, and another to see that the overall heart output meets demand, i.e. it can beat more quickly and with greater volume if demand increases as in running for a bus, or charging upstairs. Also, as we have said the heart is under emotional control so that sudden fear, etc., can make it 'miss a beat'. Basically the functioning of the heart is co-ordinated with the demands of the body by a complicated nervous and chemical control system. Interestingly this makes it possible to use drugs to influence both heart and blood pressure.

Clearly, disorders of this co-ordinating mechanism will cause malfunctioning of the heart and they indeed do. For instance, if the internal conducting system gets interfered with the signal from the atria does not get to the ventricles which may beat much more slowly, a condition called heart block. The converse is also true, and the atria may 'go mad' and beat too often and cause a rapid and inefficient ventricular beat – a condition called auricular fibrillation.

The last point to note about the heart is that being made of muscle which is quite thick in parts, it must, like all other muscle, have a good blood supply to bring it oxygen and the other necessary constituents of blood. Because the heart is in fact a very active organ, it has its own arterial system which comes off the aorta just beyond the aortic valves. There are two main arteries which run round what is called the base of the heart – which is in reality the junction between auricle and ventricle. Because these initially 'run round' in this way to right and left, these were called the coronary or 'crown' arteries. It is blockage of these vessels by blood clotting inside them that causes coronary thrombosis – thrombosis meaning formation of a blood clot.

As a blocked vessel cannot transmit blood, the muscle supplied by this vessel literally goes hungry and dies from oxygen starvation, this is called infarction.

Thus coronary artery thrombosis causes heart muscle infarction: infarctde or dead muscle cannot function so the coronary thrombosis causes the heart either to stop entirely – if it is a massive one – or to lose power and function badly.

As the left ventricle is the main power-house of the heart, it is likely to be, and indeed is, most vulnerable to blockage of its fuel supply. Clearly the effect of the blockage will depend on where it is. Blockage or thrombosis high up the vessel is more likely to destroy much more heart muscle than one lower down a branch vessel. What in fact determines the severity of a coronary is the degree of anastomosis and overlap between the areas supplied by any two vessels.

One last thing about the function of the heart. The adult body contains about ten pints of blood (depending on height and weight, etc.), so that women and children have less blood than large men. This is constantly circulating through the arteries, into tissue capillaries and then back into the veins and thence back to the heart and lungs. Circulation takes about two minutes and the heart beats 65–75 times a minute at rest.

When the left ventricle contracts its content of about 70 ccs of blood is squeezed rapidly into the aorta or main vessel which in an adult is about $\frac{3}{4}$ inch in diameter. The aorta, and all other arteries, have elastic walls, which are stretched by the blood suddenly being forced into them, the recoil from this stretching helps to push the blood round to the periphery. Clearly to circulate at all it must be under pressure. In fact doctors recognize two levels of blood pressure, one the pressure of ejection which is known as the systolic pressure and one which is the pressure of arterial flow following the elastic recoil in the arterial wall. This is known as the diastolic pressure. Obviously systolic pressure is greater than diastolic and blood pressure is expressed as systolic/diastolic or say 128/74 when mentally and physically relaxed.

Surprisingly it is difficult to define normal blood pressure because it varies with age, body build, obesity and so on. But for a young adult it should be about 130/80 when mentally and physically relaxed.

The heart and blood vessels thus form a closed hydraulic pumping system very like that which works any modern domestic heating system. The only point about it is that it maintains itself without the help of an engineer or mechanic, works continuously and has a built-in control system that equates supply and demand. It may need no maintenance – but it does require taking care of – for reasons that will be seen in a later chapter.

Muscles which form the main mass of the body do the work that maintains the body's posture and move it about. To do this they require fuel and energy and if they have to work hard they clearly require more fuel. Just as a car requires more accelerator and a lower gear to go up a hill, so does a muscle require more blood to run for a bus or carry a suitcase upstairs.

29

If more blood is required the heart must beat faster and more strongly and as more blood is circulating faster more oxygenation will be required.

Thus when activity is undertaken the pulse rate goes up and breathing becomes deeper and more rapid. It is in fact limitations of these two systems that limits activity. Equally, training of these two systems improves the potentiality for activity. Suitable mechanisms exist for controlling and co-ordinating these needs.

Here it is worth noting that the heart being muscular is likely to work better if it is kept in training and not cluttered up with fat. This is one reason why coronary heart disease is commoner in sedentary people.

Disorders of the heart

Two possible causes of heart disease have already been mentioned: one a disruption of the hearts' own conducting system which causes an abnormality of rhythm which in turn effects efficiency and output. Disorders of rhythm are not uncommon and they may in fact be due to primary disruption of the conduction system, or to secondary disruption, as when for instance a coronary thrombosis destroys a part of the network and, lastly, alterations which arise in the chambers themselves, usually as an end result of prolonged overwork. It is in these last two types of case that electronic pacemakers and the kind of monitoring that is done in intensive and coronary care units, are so helpful and indeed life-saving.

Second, destruction of the heart muscle by removal of its blood supply – as in a coronary thrombosis.

We also mentioned that the heart was unable to function properly if the pressure gradient was broken by a hole in the septum – causing a venous heart or blue baby.

On the same mechanical basis we can postulate that there might be two other broad causes of disorder, one arising from disease of the valves and another from an increased load on one part of the circuit or system.

Before discussing these in a little more detail one must make a general biological point, which is that a muscle or group of muscles will increase in size to meet a new or increased load. The same is true of the heart.

Thus if there is a defect in one of the valves or an increase in the resistance of one of the circuits – pulmonary or systemic – the muscle of the chamber concerned will increase in volume in an attempt to meet the new demand. This increase, or hypertrophy as it is called, may deal with the situation for a time, but sooner or later the over-burdened heart wears out and goes into failure. Clearly the symptoms of failure will depend on whether it is the right or the left side of the heart that has failed.

Valvular disease is much less common than it used to be, rheumatic disease, infections and birth abnormalities, were the main things which affected the valves. If they were destroyed or weakened they either leaked or became blocked. In either case the relevant heart chamber had to work harder to overcome the disability. It might go on for years, but sooner or later heart failure set in. In the old days nothing much could be done about this, except to treat the infection. Now, of course, artificial valves can be fitted and blocked valves cut out or stretched.

It has been said already that lung infection interferes with oxygenation – either acutely in pneumonia or chronically in bronchitis or emphysema. In either case the blood cannot get round the lung and the work load on the right heart is increased. Ultimately heart failure and oxygen shortage makes life impossible.

Similarly, if the resistance in the peripheral circulation goes up the left heart must expand its work capacity to meet it. If an unfit person takes exercise a normal, beneficial and entirely physiological expansion happens. This is why an athlete's heart tends to be bigger than a clerk's. But if the load is abnormal pressure goes up to meet it, and if the abnormal or pathological demand is maintained, high blood pressure results, and this may be followed by heart failure. This is discussed in more detail in Chapter 8.

People tend to think that medicine is a mysterious cult practised by near magicians. We hope that this explanation of how the heart works will support our contention that there *are* reasons for most things in medicine. The more individuals understand, then the better they can co-operate in treatment – which should also be based on reason.

4 Examination and assessment of cardiac function

Have you ever wondered what the doctor discovers when he thumps your chest and listens through his stethoscope? With the knowledge about cardiac function that has been derived from the previous chapter it should be possible to understand the activities that underlie the medical procedures which constitute the examination and assessment of the cardiovascular system.

Before going into this in any detail, one must make the point that medicine is a very traditional profession and that much of what used to be necessary 25 years ago is done much better by machines and devices. Thus while heart size can be percussed by laying a finger on the chest and hitting it in a special way to get a resonance, x-rays give a much more accurate assessment of the size and shape of the heart. Doctors are creatures of habit – so, of course, are patients – both expect certain things to be done, and done they tend to be. There is still a lot of relatively useless ritual in clinical medicine.

The first thing a doctor does is to take or feel the pulse at the wrist. Here the main artery which runs down the arm to the hand is just under the skin. The pulse wave coming down from the aorta can be felt and its rate counted. As we have said, this is usually 65–75 beats a minute. If the heart is overworking – or if there is a fever – the rate will be raised. Also it will be noted for regularity (again we have said something about the cause and significance of irregularity) and also the thickness of the artery wall can be assessed for 'hardening', see Chapter 5. It is also possible, with experience, to make a rough guess about the blood pressure – but this is interesting rather than reliable.

Next the doctor percusses the chest to outline the size of the heart. If you hit a hollow wall with joists in it, there will be two sounds, one hollow and the other solid. As heart tissue is more solid than lung tissue, percussion over it makes a different noise. Similarly solid lung, with say pneumonia, makes a different sound to normal air-containing lung. This gives a very rough measure of the size and position of the heart.

Using his stethoscope – which is a very simple listening system – the doctor can hear the heart beating. He checks on the rate and rhythm and listens over the four main sets of valves (right and left auricles and ventricles) to hear if they are functioning normally. If they are leaking or blocked the blood going through them makes an abnormal noise. Because the function of heart and lungs is inter-related it is also useful at this time to assess the lungs by the same process of listening and percussion.

The next step is to measure the blood pressure which is, in fact, measured against a column of mercury in a gadget called a sphygmomanometer. We have already seen that blood is pumped round the arteries under pressure and that arteries have elastic walls which can be compressed – as one does in First Aid to stop bleeding.

If then one applies a pressure to the limb which is higher than that of the circulating blood, the artery will be blocked and no blood can flow through it. If one listens over the artery, again with a stethoscope, one should be able to hear the blood coming through as the pressure is released. If the pressure can be measured at the point where flow recommences one should be recording the systolic pressure.

All this is what happens when blood pressure is taken. A pneumatic cuff is placed round the arm. It has a tube coming out of it to a rubber bulb or pump and another to a column of mercury which measures the pressure in the cuff.

34

The cuff is blown up to a pressure greater than that of the blood circulation – say 200 mms of mercury. The air is then let slowly out of the cuff through a simple valve while listening over the artery just below the elbow. It has to be a fairly large artery, the one at the wrist is big enough to count and feel, but too small to listen to. The blood coming back through the artery makes a characteristic sound, and the pressure at which this occurs can be read off the mercury column. This will give the systolic pressure, say 135.

If the listening process is contained for a little and pressure reduction maintained, another set of sounds is heard which roughly corresponds to the diastolic pressure – say 85. This will give a blood pressure reading of 135/85, which would be normal for a middle-aged adult.

Such a procedure is simple applied physics and hydraulics. It is a quick, simple and reasonably accurate examination which gives the basic information about an individual's cardiac function. Search can also be made for signs of cardiac failure such as distended veins and swollen ankles – but there are also other causes of these abnormalities.

By looking into the eye with a special optical instrument called an ophthalmoscope, it is possible to see 'naked' blood vessels on the inside of the eye. It can be decided whether or not they are thickened and tortuous and if they are compressing the thinner walled veins.

This completes the clinical examination of the heart. If more information is required more sophisticated methods have to be used. There are two main ones, the x-ray and the cardiograph.

X-rays penetrate the tissues and will cast shadows or reflections on to a photographic film. As different tissues have different densities, hard tissues can be made to stand out against soft ones, or hard areas like lung cancers, shown against the normally translucent lung field.

Chest x-rays were primarily for showing changes in the lung

fields – cancer, tuberculosis, pneumonia, bronchitis and so on. But the heart also shows up as a hard shadow and by taking standardized pictures one can, very accurately, measure its overall size and shape and hence pick up abnormalities and any enlargement of one chamber. This, in conjunction with the other finding, serves as a cross-check and confirmation.

It is possible, by using special techniques, to measure the pressure changes inside the heart and see whether or not these are abnormal. A hollow tube called a catheter is passed up a vein into the heart and its position controlled by x-ray. This sort of assessment is used to decide the need for cardiac surgery, because as we have said, leaking valves or septal holes upset the normal pressure gradients.

Using a rather similar technique, it is possible to put x-ray opaque dye into the coronary arteries and see whether or not they are narrowed. But these two examinations are very complicated and can only be done in special centres and by experts.

The most useful and generally used method of finding out about the heart is the electrocardiograph which is simple and quick to use and requires no more than a recumbent patient. We have already seen that there is a conduction system inside the heart which co-ordinates the contraction of the muscle making up the four chambers. Electrical changes occur in a muscle when it contracts and when an impulse passes down a nerve. By tracking or recording the 'flow' of these changes it is possible to, as it were, map the distribution of the waves of contraction and relaxation.

An electrocardiograph is a piece of very sensitive electronic equipment which literally maps out the spread of the 'heart-beat wave' through the muscle. As the heart is a hollow muscular sphere one can, by taking readings from a number of directions, map out the function of the heart muscle. Usually twelve different readings are taken, and these are drawn out by a pen on to specially sensitive paper. These are called the ECG leads.

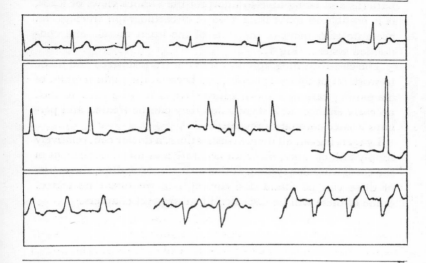

Fig. 4.

Electrocardiograms. Three tracings to illustrate the way in which the ECG can help in the detection and diagnosis of heart disease. The first line shows 3 leads from a normal ECG. The second line shows the same 3 leads from a man with advanced heart disease, hypertension and coronary thrombosis. The third line shows a disorder of conduction called left bundle branch block. The left ventricle contracts after the right resulting in a slurring of the tracing.

If this is possible in a normal heart, it is equally possible in an abnormal heart. Thus if the conduction system is damaged there will be delay in transmission, which will give a different picture. Equally, if one part of the heart is enlarged the transmission picture will be skewed in the direction of the enlargement. Similarly, if part of the muscle is destroyed by a recent coronary infarct, or replaced by scar tissue, as in an old infarct – the picture will be different. By knowing the normal and abnormal

37

patterns and being able to interpret the various views or leads, it is possible to make from a series of cardiograph tracings, an accurate assessment of the state of the heart muscle and conduction system. (Fig 4).

The electrocardiograph now that it is transistorized and made to work off ordinary batteries, has become the main method of diagnosing cardiac abnormalities. It can also be used to pick up early changes at a stage when they can be treated and perhaps a later coronary prevented.

By carrying out all these investigations, a doctor can, relatively simply and cheaply, make an accurate and useful assessment of the cardiovascular system. If there are abnormalities, the causes of these can be found and appropriate treatment instigated. Some of these will be discussed in subsequent chapters.

5 Coronary thrombosis and high blood pressure

The dependence of the heart muscle on a good blood supply and the way in which it gets this through the coronary arteries, has already been described. And it has been implied that reduction in the blood supply will impair the function of the heart.

Arteries vary in size from the aorta which has a lumen larger than many garden hoses, but thinner walls, to very much smaller vessels with relatively thicker walls and a much narrower lumen. Obviously, the smaller the lumen and the slower the blood flow the more likely the vessel is to block – just like the slow-running jet of a carburettor.

Two factors make for the blocking of an artery, firstly any disease or abnormality in its wall which decreases the size of the lumen and, secondly, an increased tendency on the part of the blood to clot or become solid.

Blood clotting is an extremely complicated biochemical process designed primarily to stop bleeding when the integrity of the vascular system is broken and blood allowed to escape. Thus, if you cut your finger a scab of congealed blood is formed which stops further bleeding. This is a useful and indeed essential protective mechanism. When it does not work, as in a disease called haemophilia, considerable and often fatal bleeding will occur.

But, less fortunately, if blood stagnates in any quantity, that is if the flow rate is reduced, there is also a tendency for the natural clotting processes to occur and for the vessel to become blocked. This process is also affected by changes in the blood chemistry which raise or lower the clotting-time. A raised blood fat (cholesterol) level is one of the factors which sometimes does this.

Blood vessels are subject to wear and tear and become diseased like all the other body tissues. They have a fine, smooth, epithelial lining which is essentially protective and allows the blood to flow smoothly. If this lining is disrupted by underlying disease, the blood flow is interfered with, local clotting may occur with a resultant 'scab' forming. Arterio or athero sclerosis is a disease of the artery wall in which fat – or cholesterol – is deposited under the lining. Diseased arteries are thus thicker than normal and, because of the damaged epithelial lining, tend to have narrower lumens. This means that they are more likely to get blocked by a thrombosis. This is what happens in a coronary thrombosis.

The coronary vessels are diseased, become narrowed and then quite suddenly get blocked, by a continuing narrowing and thrombosis. If the blockage is complete the muscle supplied will die. If it is incomplete the muscle may have an adequate blood supply at rest, but inadequate when it is under a load. A muscle without enough blood is said to be ischaemic: a heart with a poor blood supply is similarly called ischaemic and has coronary insufficiency. This can often be seen on a cardiograph or a special exercise or effort cardiograph. Damaged arteries can also be shown up by an arteriogram as described in the last chapter.

This then is the pathological basis of coronary artery disease, possible causes of it will be discussed further in Chapter 7.

If an untrained person indulges in unwanted exercise he is likely to get cramp or a stitch. This is pain arising from a muscle or group of muscles which temporarily do not have enough blood supply to bring in the right amount of energy and oxygen and to remove waste products arising from the work. Once work is stopped, by the pain, blood flow catches up and all is well again.

An ischaemic heart functions in just the same way, when it runs out of blood it gets painful cramp. This is a special sort of pain called angina. It limits the amount of work the heart can do and a rest period is required before the sufferer can go on working. The anginal pain limits physical activity and patients with this condition can, and often do, live for years. For some reason the arterial disease is somewhat different and the vessels have less tendency to thrombose – but they usually do in the end.

One of the changes that occur in physical training is that the blood supply to muscles increases by the opening up and enlargement of new or smaller arteries. This is called the collateral circulation and is possible because there is an alternative blood supply from the overlap of branching vessels. This is rather like finding an alternative route on a road or railway system, or through a series of telephone exchanges.

Unfortunately the arteries supplying the heart tend to be 'end arteries', which means that there is very little overlap in the areas some of them supply. This means, of course, that when one is blocked there is no hope for the muscle in the area supplied. In the rest of the body there is nearly always, except in parts of the brain, an alternative supply which can be brought into use. This lack does make the heart and the brain very vulnerable to vascular damage.

When heart muscle is infarcted – see Chapter 3 – it dies and is replaced by scar tissue. If the area of damage is large the heart is unable to function and the patient dies, either immediately or within a few hours. This is a form of heart failure and is a common cause of sudden death. If, however, the damage is not fatal and the heart able to carry on, the damaged area will be replaced in the ordinary process of repair, by scar tissue. This obviously leaves a weakened heart and a permanent scar that can be seen on the cardiograph.

If damage is minimal the residual muscle will take up the load and after some months the patient may be back to normal.

Whether or not he gets a further attack depends on the state of the coronary arteries, the load the heart has to carry in terms of weight and blood pressure and a number of other factors such as stress, smoking and cholesterol. About one in three coronaries are fatal and many people may live for 20 or more years before having a further attack. They may die of something quite different before this happens. One coronary is not a death sentence, particularly if the predisposing causes are dealt with.

One last point about arteriosclerosis, it is a generalized disease that may involve all the arteries in the body. To some extent it is a natural and inevitable age change. Arteries tend, in a lot of people, men and women, to get thicker, harder and less elastic with age. To this extent at least coronary thrombosis is a disease of older people and may be regarded as a 'normal' way of dying. As we shall see, it is in these cases often associated with raised blood pressure.

But when coronary thrombosis occurs in younger people, below 60, it is often a disease which is confined to the coronary arteries and is not associated with generalized arteriosclerosis. This makes it a unique and interesting, as well as an important condition. Recent research work has shown that arteries as a whole and the coronaries in particular, start to show these age changes very early in life. For instance, young American soldiers being killed in the Korean war were found to show arterial changes. Whether or not these would go on to cause early thrombosis one does not know – but it is suggestive.

There is also some evidence to suggest that the early changes of fatty infiltration can clear up when blood cholesterol is lowered. The next 10 years will bring a greater increase in our knowledge of the natural history of coronary thrombosis.

HIGH BLOOD PRESSURE

This is surprisingly more of a medical mystery than coronary thrombosis. It is a matter of common hydraulic physics that if a given volume of liquid has to be pushed through a pipe a certain pressure will be required to achieve a given flow rate. If the calibre of the tube is decreased a considerably higher pressure will be needed (16 times greater pressure if the radius is halved).

Playing with an adjustable garden hose or domestic tap will easily demonstrate the principle involved.

Exactly the same rules apply to the arterial system. If the blood vessels become reduced in size by disease or nervous spasm a higher pressure is required to maintain the circulation. This means that the heart has to work harder to achieve this. And, as we have seen, if the demand for higher output persists the heart responds by thickening up its muscle and becomes, as we say, hypertrophied. Once it does this it is likely to go on working at a higher pressure.

If this high pressure is maintained for any length of time another set of changes sets in. All the arteries are exposed to this raised pressure to which they react by thickening their walls and losing their resilience. In this way a vicious circle between the heart and arteries is set up and this is one way in which arteriosclerosis can be caused.

Certain organs like the kidneys are essential to life and thus must have a good blood supply. If their vessels are diseased, as they may be in nephritis, the blood pressure goes up to overcome this, and generalized hypertension may set in. More will be said about what happens in hypertension in Chapter 8.

The mystery about the disease is what changes happen first in uncomplicated hypertension. Is it the heart which suddenly starts working at higher pressure, or are there primary changes in the arteries to which the heart responds? No one knows the answer to this problem, but we do know that the chemical and nervous control of blood pressure is extremely complicated and that a number of factors are involved. For instance, emotional stress, such as losing one's temper or having a row with a traffic warden, obviously puts up blood pressure. Similarly, tense and highly strung people tend to have high pressures and placid, peaceful people low pressures. Thus it can at least be postulated that prolonged stress could initiate the changes that make the vicious circle permanent. We also know that blood pressure is, in a lot of people, very labile, which means that it is up and down from minute to minute. This could be the starting point for what is called essential hypertension. Again we need to know a lot more about the natural history of the disease. But it is worth noting that much hypertension is now treatable, and if it is picked up early, simple measures may keep it down. More will be said about this later.

6 Some common diseases

Although this book is mainly about the prevention of cardio-vascular disease it would be incomplete without some brief mention of the other common forms of illness and disability. But to try and do this without writing a short textbook of medicine involves some necessarily arbitrary selection. In this respect it must be realized that many of the more dramatic conditions which cause long-term disability, like multiple sclerosis, muscular dystrophy, spasticity and so on, are statistically relatively uncommon. Long-term or chronic mental upset which may be a congenital defect (present at birth) or acquired later in life, like schizophrenia, severe depression or alcoholism, are outside our present scope.

In the first chapter we listed the common causes of death in men and women of various ages. These fell into four main groups: Accidents, Respiratory Disease, Cancer, Heart Disease and perhaps a fifth miscellaneous group, which includes a number of other less common conditions.

Cancer has a sinister reputation with the general public and is commonly but often unreasonably regarded as a death sentence. Because of this doctors and relatives get involved in a conspiracy of silence and deceit to avoid using the awful word. This means that no one hears about the cancers that are successfully cured and that people with symptoms that they think might be cancer, delay seeking medical advice – often with disastrous results. Thus the woman with breast cancer – which starts as a small often painless lump in one breast, who puts off seeing the doctor, is like the man who overindulges, loading the dice against survival. Early breast cancer, defined as being confined to the breast, has a five-year survival – or cure rate of over 85 per cent. That is over 85 per cent of people picked up and treated early are likely to be cured. Whereas if treatment is delayed until the condition has spread beyond the breast, the survival rate is very much lower.

Much the same is true of the other cancers common in women – those of the uterine (womb) body and cervix. The early diagnosis of these conditions is discussed in Chapter 9. The common cancers in men and women and their relative mortality rates were given in Fig. 2.

Respiratory disease

Chronic bronchitis is probably the biggest single cause of lost time and long-term disability for employed men in Britain. It is a chronic infection of the lungs which destroys the respiratory lining and interferes with the uptake of oxygen by the blood. Apart from this the infection causes sticky secretion, like the pus in a boil, to collect. This has to be got rid of by coughing.

Chronic bronchitis results from a variety of factors, such as climate, economic conditions, dusty environment as in the mines, but above all by cigarette smoking. Much can be done to palliate it, especially if it is caught early, the infection treated and the irritant removed. The man – woman – who has a cup of tea and a good cough for breakfast, ought certainly to stop smoking.

Asthma is another condition with symptoms rather similar to chronic bronchitis, but here there is a difficulty in breathing caused by spasm of the lung tubes which stops the air getting through. Prolonged over years this causes changes not unlike chronic bronchitis. Asthma is thought to be an allergic or sensitivity condition but there is also a large stress element in it. It often starts in childhood and the parent/child relationship may play a part in its causation. It is often related to eczema and migraine which are also stress conditions.

Hernia or rupture

This is a common condition in which a small portion of the contents of the abdomen get pushed out through a muscular weakness in one of the canals leading from the abdomen to the genital region. It is treatable by surgery and cure is usually complete. Although it may cause little disability, a hernia should be treated because not only will it tend to get bigger, once the canal has been stretched, but also the contents may later get stuck and the hernia become strangulated. This can be dangerous as it causes intestinal obstruction.

Hernias can be held back by a truss which is literally a plug held over the weak canal by a steel spring, but they are much better mended surgically so that the sufferer can get back to full muscular activity.

Hernias in children are due to a congenital opening or weakness of the canal, and in adults they are due to muscle weakness and stretching. Obviously if there is any tendency to rupture, coughing and straining is likely to make it worse. As the canal is bigger in men than women (because the testicles are in the scrotum in men and the ovaries inside the abdomen in women), ruptures are much commoner in men.

Varicose veins and hæmorrhoids (piles)

Varicose veins are a dilation and swelling of the normal veins in the leg. Because the valves are weak the veins cannot support the column of blood between the ankles and the heart, and the back pressure dilates and expands the veins. Enlarging may cause pain and swelling of the leg, they may, being just below the skin, get damaged and bleed alarmingly. (This bleeding can always be stopped by lying down and raising the leg in the air on a chair back or on the wall. A tight bandage is then applied.)

Also the skin over the veins gets damaged and varicose ulcers occur. Ulcers are commoner in women than in men.

Varicose veins are common in women perhaps because of the raised venous pressure that occurs during pregnancy. The veins in the pelvis being compressed by the expanding womb.

Piles are varicose veins of the anal canal, once established they get pinched in the canal and swell even more.

Both conditions are best treated by surgery, which in skilled hands is virtually always successful.

Rheumatism

This is an omnibus phrase used to cover the multitude of aches and pains which arise from bones, joints and muscles. It covers a wide range of conditions from trivial fibrositis to the debilitating rheumatoid arthritis which can be totally disabling. So-called rheumatism and muscular pain is a major cause of lost time. Much of it reflects postural or muscle tension and is likely to have a large stress element. It causes a great deal of disability and is difficult to treat. It is fully described in another book in this series.*

Arthritis

Strictly speaking this means inflammation of the joints, which is true of rheumatoid arthritis and other acute infections. But the commoner 'creaky joint' arthritis is better regarded as a wear and tear condition causing rusty joints which creak and hurt when they are moved. It tends to come on with age and involve the larger weight-carrying joints. Joint injury early in life will obviously predispose, and being overweight increases the strain on already damaged joints. Arthritis of the spine, hips

* *Arthritis and Rheumatism* Dr. W. S. C. Copeman.

and knee is not uncommon and may require surgical treatment. Artificial hip joints are being rapidly developed at present.

Prolapsed disc

The spinal column is an interlocked chain of bones called vertebrae, which keeps the body vertical and supports its weight. (Animals which move about horizontally have little trouble with their backs.) Not only is the spine weight-bearing but it also has to be mobile to allow bending and rotation – particularly of the head. The spinal cord from which the main nerves arise, runs down through the back of the bones in a canal. The nerves emerge through openings between the vertebrae. This means that the nerves are vulnerable to pressure if there are any bony changes which cause narrowing of the canal or openings.

Between the body of each vertebrae there is a tough elastic washer which acts as a shock absorber and allows the bones to move on each other. These washers or intervertebral discs, as they are called, take a tremendous pounding and are clearly liable to be damaged. They are attached to the edges of the vertebral bodies and if this attachment gets weakened it may give way and allow the more viscous central material of the disc to protrude through the weak area. Clearly if this happens in the direction of a nerve canal the nerve will be pressed on and pain will be experienced. Equally clearly the protrusion may pop in and out so that symptoms come and go.

Not all back pain is due to discs, but if it is, and simple measures do not control it, surgical removal may be necessary. Obviously disc damage is more likely in the mobile parts of the spine, i.e. the neck and lumbar regions.

Disc injury is related to use and abuse of the back, proper methods of lifting and handling heavy weights will help to minimize the chances of trouble. Similarly, and this applies to arthritis in general, the stronger the muscles and the more mobile the joints are kept, the less likely there is to be damage or pain.

In this respect a course of exercises which strengthens the muscles is likely to be better than a spinal jacket or belt which attempts to fix the joints and weaken the muscles. Active physiotherapy can be a great help in most types of muscle and joint pain.

This is discussed further in the section on exercise.

Dyspepsia, indigestion and 'stomach ulcers'

A dyspeptic-looking individual is one who looks sour and bitter and in constant pain. He or she is often at odds with their digestive system which rebels by causing constant or intermittent pain, wind, heartburn and so on.

We all get acute tummy upsets from time to time, which result from acute infections, dietary indiscretions, or a plain hangover. More serious dyspepsia results from disorganization of the smooth working of a complicated system which has to take in solid and liquid food, break it down into simple substances that can be absorbed and used by the body and then eliminate the residue as urine or faeces.

Anything that upsets the system, and many things can, will result in various forms of indigestion, which can range from trivial wind or turbulence to serious ulceration of the stomach, duodenum or large intestine. Pain from the digestive tract arises in three ways, (1) abnormal acidity escaping from the stomach into the gullet – heartburn, or from ulcers, (2) distension by wind or (3) the colicky pain which arises from the intestines trying to squeeze its contents on, either too fast or past some obstruction.

Doctors should always be consulted about abdominal discomfort which does not get better in a day or two or respond to simple alkalis. But it can be seen that because of its nature and the complicated co-ordination required in digestion – the digestive tract is very likely to be effected by the emotional state of its owner. This means that there is likely to be a large stress element in all types of dyspepsia. Symptoms can be relieved by medicine and ulcers removed by surgery, but unless the personality environment cause is dealt with, complete cure is less likely.

Gynaecological complaints (women's diseases)

The female reproductive system and the monthly cycle which controls it, is again a complicated system which can easily get out of phase. Equally it can be damaged mechanically in childbirth or infected to cause an irritating discharge. Painful or irregular periods are probably one of the commonest causes of disability in women. And for obvious reasons people are often reluctant to seek help and advice about these disorders. This is a pity because the great majority of them are easily and successfully treatable.

Skin diseases

The skin is an extremely complicated structure which not only has to stand up to a wide range of insults from the environment, but also is a sense organ and plays a major part in heat regulation. It is thus not surprising that it is liable to infection and upset. Skin diseases are a common cause of disability. As it is through the skin that we receive a lot of our information about the outside world and convey the 'sensation' of ourselves to others, it is not surprising that there is a large stress or emotional element in skin diseases. Many of which are difficult to treat effectively.

A reactive skin – and blushing and pallor are emotionally based skin reactions – or a weak digestion are often signs that the individual cannot come to terms with the problems of life.

Diabetes

In this disease the metabolism of sugar, derived in the body from carbohydrate, is disturbed. Sugar level in the blood rises and sugar is passed in the urine. If it is severe, the biochemical balance of the blood is upset and coma may supervene.

The disease is largely caused by an upset in the mechanism whereby a hormone called insulin, which comes from special tissue in the pancreas, controls the blood sugar level. Early symptoms of the disease include thirst, weight loss and the passing of increased amounts of urine.

The disease is 'suspected' on the basis of sugar in the urine and is hence susceptible to screening tests; indeed, several community surveys for diabetes have recently been successfully done. Sugar in the urine must then be checked by a blood sugar measurement because a 'leaking' kidney can give a positive test without it necessarily being diabetes.

The disease is eminently treatable. In mild cases, restriction of carbohydrate may be all that is necessary. Failing this, oral anti-diabetic pills or insulin injections will be needed. Treatment will have to continue for life – but diabetics can and do lead long and useful lives with little incapacity.

It is a disease which is more common in old people and thus found more frequently in women than men.

This chapter has attempted to outline some of the commoner causes of ill health and disability. It is far from exhaustive, but is included partly to explain the nature of the common conditions because many people do not realize that there are explanations for most medical conditions and partly to encourage people to get the right sort of advice about dealing with them. Many people could be helped by a greater understanding of what is wrong with them and what might have caused it.

7 Causes of coronary thrombosis

We have already described the main anatomical and pathological features of the coronary arteries and what happens when they get blocked by a thrombosis or blood clot. The arteries supply the muscles of the heart which dies if it is deprived of its blood supply. Blockage we said arose from a combination of two factors: firstly, disease in the artery wall which decreased its elasticity and reduced the size of the lumen. Secondly, possible changes in the chemistry of the blood which made it more likely to clot. This is, of course, the basis of anti-coagulant treatment for thrombosis – in the hope that increasing the clotting-time, or thinning the blood will reduce the chances of a recurrence.

Both conditions are related to changes which affect the whole body – or all the blood and blood vessels, and may be regarded as generalized rather than local disease – but in the type of coronary thrombosis that occurs in younger people the pathological changes may surprisingly be confined to the coronaries. This may make it a specific disease as it were on its own.

It was also pointed out that hypertension produced changes in both the heart and the arteries which could also predispose to coronary thrombosis. But the majority of coronaries in younger people are probably not associated with hypertension.

Against this background, what then are the factors which seem to predispose, or make it more likely that an individual will get a coronary. In considering this problem the first point to be clear about is that coronary thrombosis is multifactorial in origin. By this we mean that a number of factors are influential and that in any given person one or more may predominate, whereas in the 'next man' others may be more important. It must also be realized that much of our knowledge in this field is preliminary and that the devious chain of cause and effect, and the way in which the various links in the chain interlock, has yet to be worked out in detail. This implies, of course, that the factors listed below are not given in any order of priority or importance, except for the first one which to a degree predetermines the others. It must also be emphasized that we are here talking mainly about coronary thrombosis in younger people.

(a) *Genetic*

It is a matter of common experience that some families are long lived with a string of parents who survive into their late 70s or 80s. The converse is equally true with shorter-lived families. Coronary thrombosis may be a cause of this because there is no doubt that there is a familial tendency to get this condition. Clearly it is the age at which father got his coronary which is important here, an attack at a ripe old age being much less significant than one at 55.

This does not mean that all the sons of a coronary father will necessarily be themselves affected, but it does mean that they are more likely so to be. Which means that they ought perhaps to be more prudent about living sensibly than those with a better family history. It also does not mean that people in this category will be the only ones to be affected.

(b) *Sex*

From what has been said it will be clear that we are talking mainly about men, as women tend not to get this disease until they are much older.

(c) *Diet, obesity and cholesterol*

Obesity has been described as the commonest disease in de-

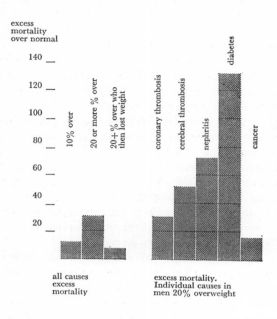

FIG. 5. Relationship between weight and mortality – as excess mortality over normal weighted. L.H. columns – 10% : 20% and 'weight losers'. R.H. column shows mortality rates from individual causes. Source: U.S. Life Insurance Companies Study.

veloped countries. This can be said with some certainty for two reasons. Firstly, because it has been firmly established by the life insurance companies, that overweight people carry an appreciably higher mortality (death) rate. Indeed this can be quantified as a 13 per cent increase in mortality for every 10 per cent overweight. Thus a man who is 20 per cent overweight is at

55

least 25 per cent or four times more likely to die young than a thinner man (Fig. 5).

Second, that in any population group well over a third will be obese or overweight, which is described as 10 or more per cent over the estimated average. The problem of weight control – which is obviously vital, is discussed in detail in Chapter 10. Mostly it is quite simply due to eating too much: which is why it is a disease of affluent societies.

Another major factor enters into the determination of weight and that is body build or somatotype. We all know thin, wiry, active people who eat a vast amount and never get fat. Equally there are those, unfortunate good converters, who seem to eat little but yet put on weight easily. The thin man is called an ectomorph and the round fat man an endomorph.

In between these two groups is the muscular, athletic, rather triangular mesomorph, who may carry an increased coronary risk for other, as yet not understood reasons.

Obesity – eating too much – influences life expectancy in a number of ways. The most important being through blood pressure. There is often a linear relationship between weight and blood pressure which goes up with weight, and can sometimes be brought down by strict weight control. In addition, the heavier person has to do more work in getting himself about than does the thinner. The less strain to which the heart, bones and muscles are exposed, the longer they are likely to go on functioning efficiently. Equally, the heart is likely to be as fat as the rest of the body.

If obesity is a reflection of diet, diet acts in another way because obviously it is concerned with the type of food that is eaten.

It is now well established, and has already been mentioned, that cholesterol or blood fat plays an important part in determining the onset of atherosclerosis. One theory is that the extra fat gets laid down or 'sucked out' into the walls of the vessels and

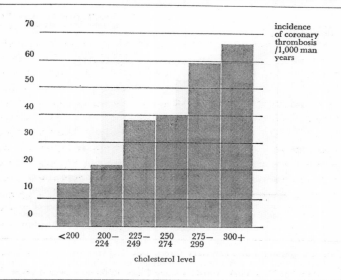

incidence
of coronary
thrombosis
/1,000 man
years

cholesterol level

FIG. 6. Cholesterol and coronary heart disease Chicago Gas Company. 1,300 men 5 year follow up.

causes a condition called atheroma. This starts off the pathological vicious circle that leads to narrowing of the vessels, it is, however, a problem still awaiting solution.

Raised cholesterol may also influence the coagulability of the blood and this acts in two ways.

Cholesterol seems to be a reflection of the amount of animal fat in the diet consumed (in meat, butter, cream, eggs, etc.). This again makes it a disease of affluence. Agrarian peoples living on a 'peasant' diet tend to have low cholesterol levels.

It is now known that individuals with a raised cholesterol level seems to carry between two and three times the coronary risk. It is also beginning to look as if lowering the level by diet

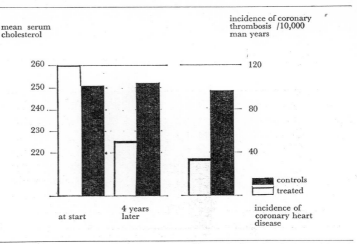

Fɪɢ. 7. Cholesterol and coronary thrombosis: showing the effect of lowering cholesterol and the reduction of coronary heart disease. (R.H. columns). Source: New York Anti-Coronary Club. 1,500 men over 4 years.

or drugs will reduce the risk – which may make this a very worthwhile exercise (Figs. 6 and 7).

There is also some evidence to suggest that there may be a link between cholesterol and smoking. Cigarette smokers appear to have higher levels than non-smokers. This could be one of the ways in which the links in the chain are interlocked.

Cholesterol levels tend to go with obesity, but not all over weight people have a high blood fat and indeed many of the tense wiry ones also have high levels. This suggests a relationship between tension, stress and cholesterol – another facet of the interlocking mechanism.

Professor Yudkin has recently suggested that refined sugar products, a form of carbohydrate, play a major part in determining coronary proneness and may also be related to cholesterol

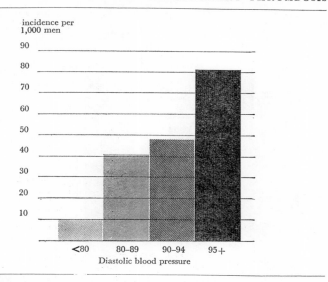

incidence per
1,000 men

Diastolic blood pressure

FIG. 8. Blood pressure and coronary heart disease Chicago Gas Company
Men 40–49, 5 year follow up.

levels. There is no doubt that affluent societies eat a lot more
sugar, this is particularly true of America where prepared foods
predominate. The chain of cause and effect here has yet to be
worked out, but a lot more will be heard about Professor Yudkin's theory over the next few years.

But it is abundantly clear that carbohydrate ought to be reduced in all our diets, particularly for children in whom it plays
a critical part in both weight and dental care. Thus sugar in
tea, coffee, ice-cream, sweet drinks, cakes and biscuits would
seem to be a food to avoid.

(d) *Blood Pressure*

This is discussed further in Chapter 8 but there is no doubt that

59

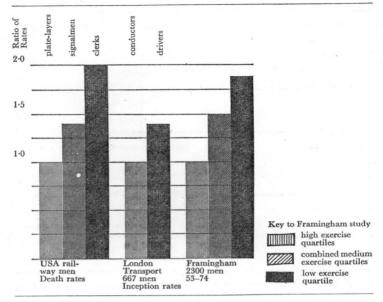

FIG. 9. Effect of exercise on coronary thrombosis rates, results of three separate studies. Note that in all cases the rate is highest in the sedentary group.

patients with high blood pressure have a greater risk of developing a coronary thrombosis (Fig. 8).

(e) *Exercise and Physical Activity*

Bus conductors have a lower coronary rate than drivers, and also lower cholesterol levels. Sedentary groups as a whole have higher coronary rates than active groups as was shown by Professor Morris some years ago (Fig. 9).

We have also seen that reasonable physical fitness 'protects' the heart in a number of ways. The heart that is used to carrying a reasonable load appears both less likely to get a coronary and should it be insulted in this way it is also better able to withstand the insult.

If you are a relatively unfit person and you rush rapidly up two flights of stairs, you will get breathless and feel your heart beating rapidly. If you do this regularly for a few days you will find that you can manage the stairs much better, with less distress. This is a very rough, but none the less meaningful measure of the improvement in your fitness and the increase in what is called cardiac reserve.

Exercise would appear to have other benefits as well. A fit person has a higher body tone than a flaccid sluggish person, blood supply to muscles is better. An active person tends to feel better and be more lively than an inactive one. He sleeps better and often seems to enjoy life more.

In simple terms, a man who walks to work across the park, feels different to one who fights his way through the tube in the rush hour. Similarly, time spent out and about in the fresh air is stimulating compared with sitting and watching the 'box'.

It could perhaps be that housework, shopping, pram-pushing, etc., being a relatively active pursuit is one of the factors which help a woman to avoid coronary thrombosis. But other factors like hormones also probably play a part.

Exercise has been described as the finest cure for anxiety. If one has a load of problems, but manages to get thoroughly physically tired, good sound sleep is much more likely.

The problems of physical fitness and how to achieve it in the course of a busy life are discussed in Chapter 12, but there is no doubt that the active man is better and feels better than the sluggish man. This does not, mean, however, and this is the difficulty with all medical and biological generalizations, that no fit men will ever get a coronary thrombosis, or that all idle men will. The late Sir Winston Churchill used to pride himself on his physical sloth.

Common sense, however, does suggest that at least half an hour a day of reasonably brisk physical activity is likely to be beneficial. It does not matter how this is taken. Games, walking, exercises, weight training – all will do and anything is better than nothing. The essence is that it should put up the pulse rate.

(f) *Cigarette smoking*

Most of the publicity about the ill effects of cigarette smoking have been conducted on the basis of its effect in lung cancer. This has now been proved to the satisfaction of most people, but as we have seen in Chapter 1, although lung cancer is a serious and indeed increasing cause of death, it rates far below coronary thrombosis as a killer of middle-aged men.

Figure 10 shows quite clearly that cigarette smokers seem to carry between two and three times the coronary risk of non-

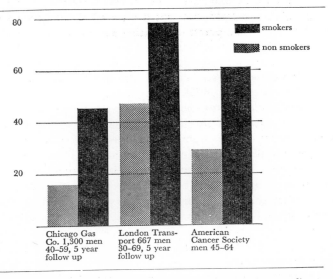

Fig. 10(a). Smoking and coronary thrombosis. Results of three studies.

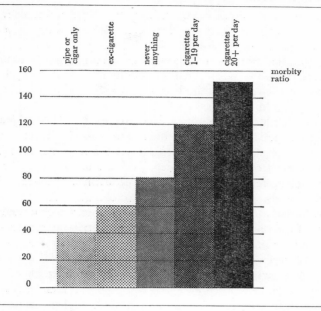

FIG. 10(b). Coronary thrombosis. by smoking, Framingham Study
2,300 men, 30–59, 12 year follow-up.

smokers. Similarly, we saw in Chapter 6 that chronic bronchitis
is a major cause of disability in Britain.

There are thus three very good reasons why it is dangerous
to smoke cigarettes:

(a) Coronary thrombosis
(b) Chronic bronchitis
(c) Lung cancer

Smoking pipes and cigars seems, so far at any rate, to be
reasonably safe. There is no evidence that filter tips provide any
appreciable protection, but there is some evidence to suggest

that the last third of a cigarette is more dangerous than the first third, presumably because of concentration of the products of combustion.

Cigarettes have a number of interesting pharmacological effects. Nicotine which is absorbed in the mouth and lungs, undoubtedly acts as a mild tranquillizer and stimulant. It is also a drug of addiction.

Inhaling a cigarette puts up blood pressure by 10–15 mm of mercury. This can be as we have seen harmful. Interestingly, smoking, probably as a direct result of the nicotine, liberates a little sugar from the liver which gives the body a mild boost – like sucking a glucose sweet. This is probably why smokers have a craving for sugar when they stop smoking.

Inhaling a cigarette produces in the lungs a high concentration of air pollution. It is, like smog, an irritant and tends to destroy the lining of the lung. This predisposes to infection and chronic bronchitis. It is possible that lung cancer is more a reflection of irritation than it is of a direct carcinogenic effect of tobacco smoke.

Interestingly, cigarettes burn at a much higher temperature than pipes and cigars, also they tend to be made of different tobacco, cured in a different way. This could give the smoke different chemical properties which might account for the safety of smoking pipes and cigars and the danger of cigarettes. There is also no hard evidence that filter tips convey any useful protection.

Currently, our society is very worried about drug addiction and mildly worried about alcoholism. But nicotine addiction is clearly both more dangerous and more widespread, and ought to be taken much more seriously. But the tax income on tobacco more or less pays for the National Health Service which makes it a difficult problem to deal with.

From all this it would appear that smoking more than ten cigarettes a day is a thoroughly dangerous activity and one which sensible people ought to avoid. It can be stopped by resolve and firmness, but addicts must realize that they will have a very rough fortnight when they do so. There is, however, an obvious pay-off for both health and finance and it is well worth the effort.

Coming back for a moment to the other predisposing factors, one can see that a man who is overweight, mildly hypertensive and has a bad family history of coronary thrombosis is literally an idiot if he goes on smoking.

The author recently saw a young man of 38 who was smoking 50 cigarettes a day, and was overweight and had a raised blood pressure of 180/110. In the year since he had last been seen his blood pressure had gone up and his cardiograph showed such obvious flattening of the tracing that it could be demonstrated to him. He left our consulting-room a frightened and a wiser man.

If he manages to stop smoking there is every reason to believe that he will return to normal or very nearly normal.

We would implore all cigarette smokers to give very serious consideration to the advisability of their addiction. It is popularly supposed that weight goes up on stopping, this is not always the case, but if it does it can be dealt with by ordinary dietary control (as described in Chapter 10) as a second-stage operation.

Two other points about smoking are worth noting, first, that the children of smokers are more likely – for obvious reasons – to become hooked. How indeed can they be stopped if they are merely copying mum and dad. Secondly, if youngsters can be kept off cigarettes until they are 21 they are much less likely to become smokers. The promise of an extra 21st birthday present may help this to be achieved. It certainly did in the author's family.

The various proprietary pills which are available to aid stopping have statistically been shown to be of little use. There is seemingly no substitute for resolve.

(g) *Stress*

The way in which an individual lives is inevitably a reflection of his personality and behaviour. This may sound a crashing platitude but when it is seen in conjunction with smoking, eating, exercise, holidays and work patterns, etc., its relevance to coronary proneness is apparent.

The harassed tortured mortal is likely to smoke too much, not take exercise and worry himself to distraction. The over-indulgent placid man will go in the same direction but for different reasons. And we have seen how mental tension affects both health in general and the cardiovascular system in particular.

The problem of stress is discussed further in Chapter 11, but it can be seen that many of the factors responsible for coronary proneness are within the control of the individual and can only, with appropriate advice, be dealt with by him. Understanding is the basis of living sensibly.

(h) *Hard and Soft Water*

Glasgow has the highest incidence of coronary thrombosis in the United Kingdom. It also has a very soft water supply. There is a certain amount of other evidence to suggest that coronary thrombosis rates are lower in hard than soft water areas. But this is really only of academic interest because there is not much one can do about this except perhaps not to buy a water softener. More may be heard of this aspect of the problem in the next few years.

(i) *Hormones*

That women get less cardiovascular disease than men, at least until they are over 60, is a proven fact. It seems that they tend not to show signs of arteriosclerosis until after the menopause (change of life). If the menopause is postponed by the use of hormone supplements it could be that the onset of cardiovascular

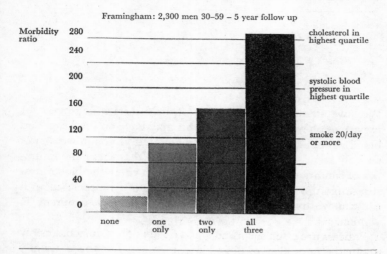

FIG. 11. Effect of multiple factors – cholesterol, smoking 20+, raised blood pressure – expressed as morbidity ratio, which is the actual number of attacks divided by the expected number. Source: Framingham Study.

disease may be even longer postponed. But this has yet to be worked out and maybe women will not want to go on menstruating for an additional ten years. It is equally doubtful that men will want to have female hormone implants to avoid coronary thrombosis. Interestingly, however, it is said that castrati and eunuchs are not coronary prone.

(j) *Multiple Factors*

All these factors interact, so that having any one only is relatively innocuous but if two or three are present very high risks result (Fig. 11).

67

8 More about blood pressure

We have already described some of the factors which make for hypertension and the effect that this may have on the heart and blood vessels. The point was also made that although we do not entirely know what causes it, we do know that there are a number of conditions like kidney disease which cause the blood pressure to go up. Because kidney infection is often associated with pregnancy, hypertension tends to be relatively common in women.

Patients are often surprised when doctors are somewhat cagey about the normality of their blood pressure. But this is usually for good reasons, because the range of variation, from person to person, and indeed in the same person from hour to hour, can vary enormously. Clearly the pressure must be adequate to maintain the circulation, fainting, for instance, is the result of low blood pressure. Equally pressure goes up with activity and down during sleep and relaxation.

It was also said that prolonged hypertension does produce changes which may, in the long run, be harmful. But doctors also know that a relatively large number of people go for years with raised pressure without any serious incapacity. This is why it is often difficult to give a definite answer to a patient.

Pressures tend to go up with age, for normal age-change reasons which we have discussed, but a raised pressure, say over 155/95, in a person under 50 is likely to be ominous, at least until it has been shown that it is not progressively increasing. Also it is clear that there are levels above which there is likely to be undesirable strain on the heart and blood vessels. In general terms the more work the heart has to do, the shorter time it is likely to go on doing it. But this rather complicated situation does make it difficult to decide what is the danger level for a given individual.

Continuously raised blood pressure has two sets of effects, one on the heart and the other on the circulation. As far as the heart is concerned, it firstly gets worn out and fails to meet the work load (heart failure sets in causing congestion on the venous side. This gives a variety of symptoms, the commonest being breathlessness, swollen ankles and congestion of the lungs) or the heart is enlarged and its coronaries are sclerotic, so that there is a greater chance of a thrombosis. Thus one sort of stroke is a heart attack, usually associated with hypertension.

The second set of effects is on the blood vessels themselves. As might be expected, these may either block or burst. Theoretically this may, and indeed rarely does, happen to any vessel anywhere. But in common practice it tends to effect the brain which gives the second type of stroke or apoplexy. Whether a vessel bursts to give a cerebral (brain) haemorrhage, or blocks to cause a thrombosis, makes little difference to the sufferer. In either case there is brain damage which is likely to cause paralysis. After a stroke there is some recovery, but nearly always a degree of permanent disability.

Because strokes are usually symptomatic of general disease they tend to recur, but a patient having a mild one may go for years without recurrence.

Diminished blood supply to the legs means, in minor form, that they do not get enough blood to meet the increased demand required for say, running for a bus or going upstairs. They react by producing a cramp-like pain which recovers with rest. This is called intermittent clandication. If one takes an x-ray of the legs of such a patient one can often see the damaged arteries because their walls contain calcium which shows up on x-ray like bone. Hence the term, 'hardening of the artery'.

Should the disease get worse, little or no blood gets through and the tissues die – a condition called gangrene, which is not uncommon in old people.

Modern surgery can do a lot for these damaged arteries which can often be either reamed out to increase their size or replaced by a graft. Cigarette smoking causes spasm of blood vessels, which is one of the ways in which it puts up blood pressure. It is thus essential that people with arterial disease should stop smoking.

High blood pressure may produce few symptoms except a thumping of the heart, or it may produce headaches and breathlessness. The former because the tension in the brain is increased, and the brain being inside a bony box – the skull – cannot expand to accommodate the tension. The latter because the already overloaded heart has no further capacity or reserve to increase its output to meet the demands of activity.

Much can now be done to deal with hypertension, particularly if it is detected early and before permanent changes have set in. Obviously the first thing to do is to reduce weight, cut smoking and slowly improve fitness. But if this does not work it may be necessary to employ long-term drug therapy. There are a number of drugs which do this and they act in a variety of ways. It is often difficult to decide which is the best drug for a given case. The results of this type of treatment are improving all the time and it is likely that with growing experience it will be increasingly possible to delay the onset of the more serious long-term effects of hypertension.

The treatment of blood pressure is also tied up with fluid and salt balance, so that pills have often to be given for this as well as the blood pressure.

Not so many years ago a damaged heart meant that the patient was advised to lead a very quiet life and undertake the minimum of physical activity. It is now realized that this was probably a mistake, and that even a damaged heart works better if it is kept in reasonable training. Once the acute stage of a coronary is over it is now usual to encourage the patient to get back reasonably quickly to a normal existence and to take graduated exercise so that after six months or so walking and golf become very possible. Indeed, they are to be encouraged because the heart will soon let its owner know – by pain or breathlessness – if it is being pushed too hard. There is no evidence that gentle exercise, taken in this way and under supervision, does any harm. Indeed, it also does a lot of good for the morale of the patient.

Palpitation – the awareness of the heart beating – is a common symptom, which may as we have said be a sign of hypertension. But it is much more common in nervous, fatigued and stressed people. So that palpitation does not necessarily mean high blood pressure, or a damaged heart.

There is a close inter-relationship between the kidneys and blood pressure. Kidney disease, such as nephritis and pyelitis, can cause raised blood pressure. This is why urine is always tested in life insurance examinations. Similarly raised blood pressure may cause kidney changes. In a small proportion of cases it may be possible to lower blood pressure by operating on the diseased kidney.

9 Early diagnosis — well person screening

Initially we were rather disparaging about what had been done in Britain to develop preventive or early diagnostic services. Perhaps to make the point we tended to underestimate what has in fact been going on in a quiet way. For instance, the school medical service, with all its faults, does manage to examine the school population at least twice during their time at school. And they do pick up a useful number of major and minor abnormalities.

In industry it has been customary for many years to carry out routine screening tests on workers who are known to be in contact with potentially dangerous substances like lead, asbestos or silica. Similarly, those who work in food handling, either at the catering or manufacturing end of the business, ought to be supervised to see that they are not disease carriers.

Tuberculosis used to be a relatively common disease, but the development of modern drugs, coupled with the early diagnostic service of mass radiography has largely abolished the disease. M.M.R. (Mass Miniature Radiography) vans are still a familiar sight outside offices, factories and town halls. M.M.R. is a classical example of 'well person' screening to pick up disease in its early stages, before it has produced symptoms.

A number of surveys have been done, in general practice and on various population groups. All of these have revealed an appreciable amount of unsuspected disease in the population examined. Professor Logan has described this as the hidden iceberg of disease. The tip of the iceberg being in the doctor's surgery and the rest being hidden in the individuals who are walking around, either with a condition which may later cause trouble — such as what is called pre-invasive cervical (womb) cancer, or with a degree of chronic disability which reduces their overall health and effectiveness.

Currently in Britain there is rapid development of clinics for doing cervical smears. Here a scraping is taken from the neck of the womb and early or pre-cancerous changes may be found. It is likely that early and simple treatment will effect a permanent cure. If all women of vulnerable age could be screened, cervical cancer might be dealt with much as has tuberculosis. A problem here is that there is a social class distribution of the condition which is more common in poor and possibly deprived people; these are sadly the ones who are most difficult to get to come for screening. There is thus a tremendous health education problem to be launched before screening becomes really effective.

Interestingly, some figures have recently been published from Scotland, which has pioneered this type of screening, suggesting that over the last ten or so years, it has succeeded in bringing down the death rate from cervical cancer in the local population.

Breast cancer in women is another condition in which the prospects of improving the cure rate by screening appear to be good. If the fear of cancer could be overcome and every woman trained to examine her breasts monthly and to report any small lumps to her doctor, a dramatic reduction in the breast cancer death rate might be achieved. Early cases have at least an 85 per cent five year survival or cure rate. In late cases, in which the growth has extended outside the breast tissue, the rate goes down to less than 30 per cent. The moral of this is quite clear, and new x-ray and infra-red techniques are being developed to achieve even earlier detection.

One must not underestimate the tremendous upheaval that this will cause in the medical services. Doctors complain that they are already overworked and most hospitals have long waiting lists. But progress is only made by altering priorities, and if the rising toll of overt disease is ever to be reduced early diagnosis must be instigated.

Two points would seem to make this easier than might at first appear. The first is that the actual screening can be carried out by specially trained technicians and nurses. The second is that the extra or early treatment is likely to be easier and simpler than that required for the more florid or established disease.

In America what is called multiphasic screening is being developed. In this a battery of tests or examinations are arranged in one large room, to be carried out one after the other. Thus an individual coming for screening goes through the system and may have his vision, hearing, urine and blood chemistry all tested in about an hour and a half. The Americans being rich and technically clever, have automated a lot of this, and the Kaiser Permanente organization in California, which has pioneered this concept, runs a unit with 20 testing stations entirely staffed by nurses and technicians.

What happens is that the doctor is finally presented with a detailed profile of the individual. With this as a basis he can both pick up early signs of disease and establish a base-line for health.

A modest start has been made in this direction in Britain. Several enlightened local authorities have recently run simple screening clinics for their own rate-payers. Not only have they found there to be the expected amount of previously undiagnosed disease, but also the public has flocked to them. Indeed, they have been unable to meet the local demand.

In our own medical centre, which is primarily for business executives, we have been growing at over 30 per cent per year. In 1967 we carried out 3,500 very detailed and specialized examinations – and we found something wrong with about a third of the people we saw – a very worthwhile yield, especially in the younger people. This type of approach has an additional advantage, in that it is possible to reassure the individual that he *seems* to be in good shape. One has to be a little careful not to create a feeling of false confidence so that symptoms, like bleeding or indigestion, are minimized because they came on just after a successful or normal examination.

Critics of this approach to medicine say that this false confidence is likely to be dangerous, and they also say that all we shall do is to produce a race of hypochondriacs. But one never gets something for nothing in this life and the minimal risks of false confidence are surely better than waiting for disease to manifest itself. It seems likely to be that an informed public are going to lead the medical profession and the administrators into providing adequate screening facilities. We hope that it will soon become accepted that the regular maintenance of individuals will be regarded as just as valuable and necessary as having one's car serviced. The trouble here is, of course, that modern cars may soon need less servicing than their drivers.

In general terms, however, it can be said that pre-symptomatic diagnosis can reasonably be regarded as prudence rather than hypochondria.

If we can now come back to our main field of cardiovascular disease, it is easy to see that if a doctor is able to talk to an individual about his life and work, to examine him clinically and then to carry out a series of investigations – cardiograph, x-ray, lung function, blood chemistry and so on – he will be in a position to draw up a moderately accurate cardiovascular balance sheet. In the light of these findings he can advise the man what he ought best to do to minimize his chances of getting a coronary. It could be that nothing will be found and he can be reassured but even if this is the case, a very worthwhile base-line will have been charted, against which later change can be accurately measured. If, however, he is overweight, smokes too much and has a raised cholesterol and cardiograph changes it may be possible to help him. Similarly, if he is overworked and under-exercised, an attempt can be made to persuade him to alter his habits, which might perhaps prevent the changes occurring.

From what we have said coronary thrombosis must be regarded as a process and not an event, although obviously it is the often tragic event which counts. But by the time this happens it may be too late. It is clear that in the present state of our knowledge, regular screening, particularly of younger people in whom the earliest signs may be found, holds out the best chance of success.

It is, in fact, highly likely that the next ten years will see a revolution in diagnostic medicine. Multiphasic screening holds the seeds of early diagnosis and by having a comprehensive diagnostic clinic it becomes cheaper to do all the tests at once, than to leave the choice of tests to the whim of the doctor. Often even in quite ill people routine testing of this type throws up an unsuspected diagnosis.

Our firm advice is to encourage the public to come for periodic medical examinations and to press for the provision of adequate facilities all over Britain.

10 Nutrition

To maintain health the body needs to have an adequate intake of a large number of different constituents. It is however no less true that an excess of any of them may be as harmful as a deficiency. A well-known hazard of Arctic explorers is the severe illness caused by eating polar bear liver, which contain enormous amounts of vitamins A and D. The evils of excess weight will be clear to those who have read this far. Prolonged intake of a large excess of ordinary salt will often lead to a raised blood pressure.

The principal requirements of the body are, Calories, proteins, vitamins, essential fatty acids, minerals and trace elements and of course water. Prolonged deficiency in any of these will lead to disease and eventual death. As we have said, prolonged excess may be equally harmful. The art, therefore, is to maintain a balance. Nature is remarkably good at this and on the whole, in Britain, severe deficiency is rare and the only common excess is obesity, due to excessive Calories.

Normal Weight

This is almost impossible to define, but it is quite clear that it is not the same as average weight. A possible, though cumbersome definition is, 'the weight at which a person's expectation of life is maximal'.

This is clearly an individual approach. Certain life insurance statistics from America indicate that as a rough generalization, the mean weights of healthy individuals aged 25–30 approach this theoretical 'normal' allowing, of course, for height.

TABLE 2

AGE AND WEIGHT IN POUNDS: MEN

Height	Under 30 Average weight	Under 30 10% over-weight	Under 30 20% over-weight	30–39 Average weight	30–39 10% over-weight	30–39 20% over-weight	40–49 Average weight	40–49 10% over-weight	40–49 20% over-weight	50–59 Average weight	50–59 10% over-weight	50–59 20% over-weight	Over 60 Average weight	Over 60 10% over-weight	Over 60 20% over-weight
5' 3"	134	147	160	138	151	165	141	155	169	142	155	169	139	152	166
5' 4"	137	151	165	142	155	169	145	158	173	146	159	173	143	157	170
5' 5"	141	155	169	146	157	170	149	161	177	150	165	180	146	162	176
5' 6"	144	158	172	150	165	180	154	169	184	155	170	185	152	167	182
5' 7"	148	161	176	154	169	184	158	174	191	159	175	192	156	172	188
5' 8"	151	166	181	158	174	191	162	178	194	163	179	195	161	177	193
5' 9"	156	172	188	163	179	195	167	184	201	168	185	202	166	183	200
5' 10"	160	176	192	167	184	201	171	188	205	173	190	207	171	188	205
5' 11"	165	182	199	172	189	206	176	194	212	178	195	214	176	194	212
6' 0"	170	187	204	176	194	212	180	198	216	182	200	218	181	199	217
6' 1"	175	193	211	181	199	217	185	204	223	187	206	225	186	205	224
6' 2"	179	197	215	186	205	224	190	209	228	192	211	230	191	210	229
6' 3"	183	201	219	192	211	230	196	216	230	198	218	232	197	217	231

Average weights for age. 10% and 20% over-weight WITHOUT SHOES AND STRIPPED (if measured clothed and shod subtract 1" and add 7lb). Taken from Metropolitan Life Insurance Co. figures 1959 – adjusted for shoes and clothing. (Normal for a heavily-built person could be up to the 10% level.)

9 st	126 lb
10 st	140 lb
11 st	154 lb
12 st	168 lb
13 st	182 lb
14 st	196 lb
15 st	210 lb
16 st	224 lb
17 st	238 lb

Table 2 shows the average weights for men of various ages. Height, without shoes and weight, unclothed. A variation of 10 per cent on either side is probably acceptable.

TABLE 3

AGE AND WEIGHT IN POUNDS: WOMEN

Height ft. in.	Weights according to age period								
	15–19	20–24	25–29	30–34	35–39	40–44	45–49	50–54	55–59
4 11	110	113	116	119	122	126	129	131	132
5 0	112	115	118	121	124	128	131	133	134
5 1	114	117	120	123	126	130	133	135	137
5 2	117	120	122	125	129	133	136	138	140
5 3	120	123	125	128	132	136	139	141	143
5 4	123	126	129	132	136	139	142	144	146
5 5	126	129	132	136	140	143	146	148	150
5 6	130	133	136	140	144	147	151	152	153
5 7	134	137	140	144	148	151	155	157	158
5 8	138	141	144	148	152	155	159	162	163
5 9	141	145	148	152	156	159	163	166	167
5 10	145	149	152	155	159	162	166	170	173
5 11	150	153	155	158	162	166	170	174	177
6 0	155	157	159	162	165	169	173	177	182

Table 3 shows average weights for height figures for women
without shoes or clothes

Middle-age-spread is a truism and the increase in average weight
with age is so well known as to be often taken as normal and
acceptable. However, accurate follow-up of these middle-aged
men of 'average' weight, shows that they have a higher death rate
(particularly from diseases of the heart and blood vessels) than

their thinner colleagues. Tables 2 and 3 give these figures which may be taken as an approximation to the normal weight.

Certain people are naturally lean, they are called ectomorphic, 'normal' weight for them is about 10 per cent less than that in the tables. Certain people are naturally very muscular, they are called mesomorphic. If these people are in training (e.g. weight-lifters) they may be 15 per cent above the values in Tables 2 and 3. This weight being due to muscle rather than fat is not harmful; in middle age these men may lose the muscle and put on fat – they thus may become 'overweight' without actually putting on weight; they are then at a great risk of developing heart disease. Other people are naturally 'well rounded' and are called endomorphic, they are particularly liable to put on excess weight because they are 'good converters'.

Calories

Except for certain diseases, excessive weight is solely due to prolonged excessive intake of Calories. The calorie is a unit of heat which is defined as the amount of heat required to raise the temperature of one gram of water by one degree centigrade. This is too small a unit to be practical in medical usage, so that in all consideration of diet the Calorie is used; this is equal to 1,000 calories and is thus the heat required to raise 1 kg of water through $1°$ C (or approximately 4 lb. of water through $1°$). This Calorie is sometimes called a Kilo calorie or a K calorie or a big Calorie, much more confusingly it is often written with a small 'c' which can lead to a ludicrous error being made.

Fat is the main energy store of the body. Any energy from food which is not immediately required is converted to fat. About 9 Calories go to a gram of fat (about 4,100 to the pound). If more energy is used than is provided by the Calories in the food, then fat is burnt up. Clearly the essential to maintaining a normal weight is a full understanding of Calorie balance.

TABLE 4

THE 'EXTRA' ENERGY EXPENDITURE OF EVERYDAY ACTIVITIES. THE
FIGURES GIVEN ARE FOR AVERAGE MEN AND WOULD BE APPROXI-
MATELY 20 PER CENT LOWER FOR WOMEN. SLIGHT ADJUSTMENTS CAN
BE MADE FOR SMALL OR LARGE SIZES

	K cals/hour
Sitting	15
Standing	35
Walking (slow = 2½ m.p.h.)	120
(fast = 5 m.p.h.)	350
(5 m.p.h. up a 1/10 hill)	850*
'Light' work	20 to 220
'Moderate' work	225 to 370
'Heavy' work	375 to 550*
Typing (40 w.p.m. mechanical machine)	50 (women)
Light housework	80 to 120
Heavy housework	150 to 300
Driving	20 to 60
Playing cricket	100 to 250
Playing football	350 plus
Playing tennis	250 to 350
Playing ping-pong	100 to 250
Dancing	250 to 350
Hard gardening	250 to 350

Note. For total energy expenditure a basal figure of about
67 Cals/hour for men and 56 Cals/hour for women should
be added.*
Calorie expenditure of more than about 450 Cals/hour
should not be attempted for any length of time by men
not accustomed to it.

Calorie Expenditure

This is the debit side of the account. Like the family banking
account, it can be split into two parts – standing orders and individual payments. A certain amount of energy is required just
to keep alive. Breathing, keeping the heart beating and all the
other organs functioning and fully maintained, all require
energy. The rate at which this energy is used is called the Basal
Metabolic Rate, clearly this will depend on the size of the body.
For an 'average' man about 1,650 Calories a day are required
in this way, and for women about 1,350 Calories. These would

TABLE 5

THE EXTRA ENERGY EXPENDITURE REQUIRED TO COPE WITH DISEASE, DISABILITY, ETC.

Disease	Difference
Thyrotoxicosis (excessive Thyroid activity)	500 to 1,000 K cals/day
Myxoedema (deficient Thyroid activity)	400 to 800 K cals/day less than normal
Fevers	120 K cals/day (degree Fahrenheit of fever)
Above knee amputations of leg	Walking, etc., twice as much as normal person. Excess over resting
Pregnancy	300 K cals/day (average)
Lactation (breast feeding)	750 K cals/day

be approximately the requirements of someone who literally slept 24 hours a day.

The 'individual payments' are all the activities apart from just existing. Even a trivial extra activity such as sitting quietly reading, will have an extra energy expenditure (Table 4). Men, under extreme conditions and when well trained, may manage to work at 3,000 Cs/day above basal, but only for a few days. Diseases and disabilities may lead to an increase in normal Calorie consumption, see Table 5.

Climate also affects Calorie consumption. The Basal Metabolic Rate of people acclimatized to tropical conditions is 5–15 per cent lower than in temperate climates. However, the energy expenditure on work is not affected by warmth, or may even rise in very hot conditions. Under conditions of extreme cold increased energy consumption merely to keep warm may become important. This, however, is usually only important to Polar explorers.

Body build may affect energy consumption in apparently identical situations. This particularly affects the typical 'Pickwickian' fat boy type, or endomorph. These people are adept at doing something with the minimum possible energy expenditure. In the past this may have been an advantage, allowing

TABLE 6

THE TOTAL DAILY CALORIE CONSUMPTION IN A
CROSS-SECTION OF TYPICAL OCCUPATIONS

Occupations	K cals/day
Men:	
Retired (over 65)	2,300
Office workers–clerks	2,500 to 2,800
University students	2,900
Steel workers	3,300
Farmers	3,500
Coal miners	3,700
Women:	
Housewives	2,000
Shop girls	2,250
University students	2,300
Factory workers	2,300

these people to survive better under famine conditions. Nowadays it leads to all the disadvantages of excess weight. A study from Boston (Mass.) on girls playing tennis shows that while many were on the move 80 per cent of the time, some, the overweight, were only active for 45 per cent of the time.

To sum up this situation, Table 6 gives an average daily expenditure in various sorts of jobs. The maximum rate at which a trained fit man can work regularly is probably about 4,000 K cals/day; for short periods an expenditure of 5,000 K cals/day or more can be attained.

Calorie intake

This is the credit side of the account. All common foods except water and salt have some Calorie value. This may range from 105 K cals/lb for tomatoes to 4,200 K cals/lb for lard. There are three chemically different classes of compound which between them account for over 99 per cent of all the Calorie intake in any normal diet. These are Carbohydrates, Fats and Proteins.

TABLE 7

COMMON CARBOHYDRATES

Basic units	Double units	Multiple units
Glucose	**Sucrose** (glucose and fructose) Ordinary sugar	**Starch, Glycogen**. Both many glucose units; used as energy stores. Starch in plants and glycogen in animals
Fructose		
Galactose	**Lactose** (glucose + galactose) Sugar in milk	**Cellulose** (many glucose, linked in a different way). Holds plants together mechanically. The sugar in this is not normally available to humans for energy.

Carbohydrates

Carbohydrates chemically consist of carbon, hydrogen and oxygen only, the latter two being in the same 2:1 ratio as in water. The basic unit is a sugar molecule (chemical formula $C_6 H_{12} O_6$). Many different compounds exist with this formula and others are formed by joining two or more of the basic units together. Table 7 shows some of the more common basic carbohydrates.

Carbohydrate is very common and is present in most foodstuffs except pure oils and fats. However, some foods consist mostly of carbohydrate as their energy-containing material. These include sugar, cereals, flour, pastry, cakes, bread, biscuits, rice, spaghetti, dried fruit, baked beans, dried vegetables, potatoes, and meat extract. It is worth noting that this list includes most cheap foods which makes carbohydrates important economically. Also they are foods which are palatable, particularly to children.

Carbohydrates produce 1,800 K calories of energy per pound

dry weight. Before being too frightened by this it is worth remembering that many foods are mostly water, e.g. potatoes are nearly 80 per cent water and a pound of raw potatoes contain only 385 Calories. Many carbohydrate foods contain little or no important dietary constituents, apart from their 'fuel' content. This is why it is particularly advisable to reduce markedly the intake of these foods when attempting to lose weight. It has been shown that a high carbohydrate intake, particularly of sweets and sugar, leads to dental caries, this is especially a problem in children. It has been suggested that a high intake of these substances may predispose to developing arteriosclerosis and heart disease. While this has not yet been proved, it is another reason why the prudent man will reduce his sugar intake. It is worth stressing that marked reduction in these high carbohydrate foods may be all that is required to achieve weight control.

Fats

These also consist mainly of carbon, hydrogen and oxygen, but there is relatively much less oxygen than in carbohydrates. For this reason they have a higher Calorie value than carbohydrates, a pound of pure fat giving 4,000 Calories. There are many different sorts of fats, but all tend to have fairly complex structures. The ordinary depot (energy store) fat is called triglyceride (technically minded readers see Fig. 12).

Cholesterol is a fat with a totally different chemical structure. It is believed that people with a high level of cholesterol in their blood have an increased risk of developing coronary heart disease. Cholesterol in the blood comes partly from food (egg yolks, brains, liver, kidney, caviar and yeast are particularly rich in cholesterol) and is partly made by the body. Animal (saturated) fats are particularly liable to be made into cholesterol, while vegetable (unsaturated) fats tend to prevent this.

Glycerol		
CH_2OH	$HOOC-CH_2-CH_2-CH_3$	Butyric acid*
$CHOH$	$HOOC(CH_2)_7CH=CH(CH_2)_7CH_3$	Oleic acid**
CH_2OH	$HOOC(CH_2)_2(CH=CHCH_2)_4(CH_2)_4CH_3$	Arachidonic acid***

The acids combine with glycerol with the elimination of water to form a triglyceride. These usually have similar acids attached to the three OH groups. A mixed one like the one shown would be most unusual, this was shown to illustrate the three types of fatty acid.

   * A saturated fatty acid (found in milk and butter). Longer ones with more $-CH_2-$ groups in the chain are found mainly in animal fats.
  ** A mono unsaturated fatty acid (found in olive oil). (One $CH=CH$ group.) This type is common in vegetable oil.
*** A poly unsaturated fatty acid. (More than one $CH=CH$ group.) This is an essential fatty acid. That is, the body cannot make it for itself but depends on getting enough of it from food – like a vitamin.

FIG. 12.

There are a wide variety of other fats serving specialist functions in the body, particularly in the walls of the cells and as 'insulating material' in the brain and nerves. These fats have a much more complex structure and may include other elements such as nitrogen and phosphorus. From an energy point of view they are present in such small amounts that they can be disregarded.

Proteins

These consist of nitrogen, a little sulphur and sometimes phosphorus as well as carbon, hydrogen and oxygen. They are made up of chains of 'amino acids' joined together. They are usually folded and may be cross-linked, occasionally they may be circular. They are very large and complex, the exact structure of a very small number has only recently been worked out. In fats and carbohydrates all the energy available can be used; however in proteins, a certain amount of energy is required to digest, process, and then excrete any waste products (mostly urea): this is called the Specific Dynamic Action of the food. The amount of this varies from protein to protein. It is, however, a good generalization to accept that the available energy from protein is the same as from carbohydrate 1,800 K calories per pound.

A man can exist quite healthily without carbohydrates or fats (except for a very small amount of essential fatty acids) but prolonged deficiency of protein leads to weakness, wasting and eventual death. There is some doubt as to the minimum amount of protein required for health, the recommendation is about 1/1,000 of the body weight daily (about $2\frac{1}{2}$ ounces daily for a man or 2 ounces for a woman). However, prisoners in concentration camps managed to survive for years on smaller intakes. Children need proportionally higher amounts to allow for growth. Increased intake is required during pregnancy, lactation and many illnesses, operations or injuries.

Of the 20 amino acids found in human proteins, 9 are essential, that is, the body cannot make them for itself (though some may be more or less interconvertible). Gelatin and some vegetable proteins are rather poor in some of these essential amino acids and are called second-class proteins. Most animal protein including the protein in milk and eggs is first class (i.e. contains all the essential amino acids). It is a safe rule that half the minimum requirements should be taken as first-class proteins. Good sources of protein are meat, fish, eggs, milk, fresh kidney beans, nuts, cereals, cheese (not cottage).

In Britain, lack of protein is seldom a problem except sometimes in very faddy diets or old people living off toast and tea for years. Protein excess is usually only a problem as a source of Calories. However, as most protein foods are relatively expensive, this too is unimportant. It should also be noted that calorie for calorie, protein rich foods tend to satisfy the appetite better and for longer than fat or carbohydrate rich foods. In certain diseases special high protein or low protein diets may be helpful; these should only be taken on a doctor's advice and under his supervision.

Calorie Balance and Weight Control

The body is extraordinarily good at maintaining a Calorie balance. Let us consider an average young man of 25, weight 12 stone, doing moderate work and thus having a Calorie requirement of about 3,000 K cal/day. If his balance is very slightly out, say on average an excess of 1 per cent, he will be in credit 30 Calories a day. This works out at over $2\frac{1}{2}$ lb of fat gained in a year and a weight of nearly 20 stone by retiring age. Experience tells us that over a long period of time, even such a small imbalance of 1 per cent is seldom maintained. It is also common knowledge that a gain of one or even two stone in a year is not uncommon.

It will be clear from what has been said so far, that if you eat as many Calories as you use up, your weight will remain steady. If you eat more you will gain weight, and if you eat less you will lose weight.

The means whereby the body manages to control Calorie balance is by control of the appetite. People eat because they are hungry, thus it is important to consider the factors controlling hunger. There are two straightforward physiological mechanisms causing hunger. The first is an empty stomach, if the stomach remains empty a long time it starts contracting and it may give rise to quite severe hunger pains. Certain appetite depressants are based on this mechanism, they are merely indigestible bulk of no Calorie value which fills the stomach. Certain foods, particularly fats are digested more slowly and so lead to more prolonged hunger suppression.

The second mechanism is a reflex based on the level of sugar in the blood. As this level falls so hunger is stimulated. To take advantage of both mechanisms it is probably an advantage to spread out the daily intake over several small meals rather than having just one enormous meal a day.

Both these mechanisms are under the control of the brain and their action can be modified or even totally suppressed. In rats, artificially produced lesions in the brain will lead the animal to starve to death, even in the presence of ample palatable food; different lesions will lead to continuous eating and fantastically rapid weight gains. Man is not a rat but similar effects have been noted in sufferers from certain brain tumours. However, as well as definite anatomical lesions, these mechanisms can be affected by emotional, psychological and social factors.

There is no doubt that to many people eating is a great pleasure and gratification of pleasure is a major human drive. Further, in some people, food seems to act as a sedative and they will overeat under periods of stress because of this. However, other people react in a diametrically opposite way and lose their appetite when they are anxious. Many people are under considerable social pressures not only about how much they eat but more particularly about what they eat and when they eat it. This applies particularly to alcohol consumption which can be a very rich source of Calories.

Habits of eating are set up by years of repetition, the secret of successful weight loss is in the alteration of these patterns. This involves a complete and permanent alteration in one's eating way of life. If, for a fortnight, you live on raw carrot juice, with or without the fifty-guinea help of a health farm, you will lose $\frac{1}{2}$–1 stone of fat. However when you go back to your previous dietary indiscretions it will soon go back on. Medically speaking such 'yo-yo' behaviour is not much better than a steady degree of overweight. To make the alterations successful, they must be adjusted to each individual, to allow for his health, his prejudices, his likes and dislikes, and his social and economic circumstances.

It is worse than useless to advise a one-legged man to ride a bicycle, a Jew to eat pork or a man on the dole to eat steak. For this reason this book does not give you *the* way to lose weight, if you are to make a success of it you must work this out partly for yourself, to suit yourself. What we will do is tell you what ways are available, what their advantages and disadvantages are, and how they may be combined into a new way of life, which should be not just bearable, but enjoyable.

We have considered so far only the credit side of the balance. It is possible to lose weight by taking more exercise and eating exactly the same. As a long-term measure there is no doubt that regular exercise is very beneficial to health, apart from its possible weight-reducing effect. However, attempts to lose weight by exercise only are often unsuccessful. The main reason for this is the increased appetite induced by exercise; also a very considerable amount of exercise is required to effect a really significant weight reduction. For example, 12 hours of strenuous tennis or continuous fast walking are required to burn up 1 lb of fat. There is no doubt, however, that a programme of regular exercise, allied to dietary restrictions is the best way of losing weight and keeping fit.

Slimming Diets

More has been written on this subject than on any other aspect of 'do-it-yourself' medicine. Much of this writing owes more to the enthusiasm than to the common sense of the author. The one essential of a slimming diet is that you should eat less Calories. The logical extreme is total starvation except for water and vitamins. This does lead to dramatic weight loss; it is also a potentially risky way of losing weight and should only be practised under close medical supervision, normally as a hospital patient, and relapse is very common.

Many diet sheets produced by hospitals or dietetic books

give a 1,000 (or 800, 1,200, or 1,500) Calorie diet. These are usually well balanced and effective provided they are kept to. However, sometimes they are difficult to understand and more often they are deadly dull. Other diets are based on the total elimination of one of the major dietary components such as *No Fat* or *No Carbohydrate diets*. These too are often effective, though probably less so than a more balanced diet. They are, however, so unpalatable and awkward that many people find it difficult to stick to them. Losing weight is the easiest part of slimming, staying at a normal weight afterwards is much harder and just as important. A diet which is too extreme may allow you to lose weight but unless it is a basis for a permanent alteration in your eating habits, it is unlikely to lead to a steady maintenance of normal weight.

Many other diets have been advocated and the above objections usually apply to them with increasing force the more 'gimmicky' they get. Some of the more extreme diets may, if pursued for a long time without supervision, lead to deficiency diseases, particularly anaemia.

Recently, various products have been produced which provide a complete balanced diet of a measured Calorie value. These are perfectly satisfactory provided the maker's instructions are adhered to. I remember one lady who was most indignant that she had put on weight despite eating her slimming biscuits quite regularly. It turned out that she was eating them as well as her normal meals, rather than instead of them.

The diet we recommend is as varied as possible, the individual must decide on the details according to his tastes. All foodstuffs have been classified into 3 classes; low, medium and high Calorie. This is summarized in Table 8. The quantities recommended are those for an 'average' housewife or a very sedentary man. Smaller amounts, say 12 oz of medium Calorie foods and 1 oz of high Calorie will lead to weight loss. Larger amounts will be needed by an active man. Table 9 is a specimen menu

TABLE 8

THE CALORIFIC VALUES OF SOME LOW, MEDIUM AND HIGH CALORIE FOODS

1 Low Calorie foods (less than 20 Cals/oz)	2 Medium Calorie foods (20–70 Cals/oz)	3 High Calorie foods (more than 70 Cals/oz)
Eat as much as you like	Eat up to 1 lb a day. At least 8 oz should be of protein rich foods marked*	Eat 'tastier' amounts only no more than 2 oz per day total
FRUIT AND VEGETABLES		
All fresh fruit except those in Column 2	Bananas Avocado	All dried fruits
All fresh or canned or frozen vegetables except those in Columns 2 and 3	All canned fruits Broad beans Sweet corn Parsnips Peas Potatoes Bread Rice (cooked weight) Porridge (cooked weight)	Baked beans Potato chips or crisps All dried vegetables All nuts Biscuits Cakes 'Pasta' (spaghetti, Macaroni, etc.) Breakfast cereals Semolina Tapioca
CONFECTIONERY AND SWEETENERS		
Artificial sweeteners Saccharine Cyclamate		Chocolate Sugar (or glucose or dextrose) Honey Jam Syrup All fats and oils
DAIRY PRODUCTS		
Skim milk (1 pint/ day allowed)	Cottage cheese Eggs* Full cream milk	Butter Cheese Cream Dried or condensed milk Ice-cream
MEAT*		
	All fresh meat* Boiled, roast or grilled with the fat removed	Bacon Sausages Salami Ham

1 Low Calorie foods (less than 20 Cals/oz)	2 Medium Calorie foods (20–70 Cals/oz)	3 High Calorie foods (more than 70 Cals/oz)
	SEA FOODS	
Oysters	All fresh, canned or frozen fish*	Smoked eel Caviar
	BEVERAGES	
Tea or coffee (black, unsweetened) Calorie free squashes and soft drinks Tomato Juice Fresh or unsweetened canned fruit juice Water	All alcoholic drinks Squashes (ordinary) Sweetened canned fruit juice	Cocoa powder

TABLE 9

DAILY MENU

A suggested daily menu. *Note.* Even a small cheating on the weights of medium or high Calorie foods will lead to a weight gain rather than a loss. The column numbers refer to Table 8.

Daily allowances

(Take during the day as convenient)	Calories
1 pint skim milk	35
½ oz butter	100
½ oz sugar*	55
TOTAL	190

BREAKFAST

½ grapefruit (sugar from allowance) or 1 glass of fresh or canned unsweetened fruit or vegetable juice	40
1 egg (medium) NOT fried or 1 oz kipper or haddock	75
Grilled (NOT fried) tomatoes or mushrooms (3 oz)	25
1 slice of toast (small loaf, butter from allowance)	80
½ oz jam, marmalade, or honey*	50
Tea or coffee (milk from daily allowance, artificial sweetener)	—
TOTAL	270

Early Morning Tea, Morning Coffee, Afternoon Tea, Coffee after Lunch or Dinner are all permitted – milk from allowance, artificial sweetener or sugar, from allowance.

LUNCH

Consommé or ½ grapefruit (sugar from allowance) or fresh or unsweetened canned fruit or tomato juice	40
4 oz meat (3 medium slices or a moderately large chop, NOT fried, trim off loose fat) or portion of chicken or duck or turkey (4 oz) (this can be exchanged with the main supper course)	400
Unlimited vegetables from Column 1 (NOT fried)	50
and	(per 6 oz)
3 oz of one vegetable from Column 2	100
Fresh fruit (NOT bananas)	100
	(per 6 oz)
TOTAL	690

SUPPER

Consommé, grapefruit or fruit juice as lunch	40
4 oz liver, kidney, heart, brain or tripe (NOT fried) or 4 oz fish or shellfish (NOT dried/smoked/fried) or 2 large eggs (NOT fried)	200
Unlimited vegetables from Column 1	50
	(per 6 oz)
1 slice bread (small loaf)*	80
Butter from allowance	—
½ oz cheese (1½ oz cottage cheese)	50
TOTAL	420

Additional *	1 sherry or 1 wine-glass of wine or a single whisky, gin, rum, brandy can be taken once per day, but NO beer or cider	80

TOTAL FOR DAY	1,650

If you are a woman or a very sedentary man or if you require more vigorous weight reduction omit the items marked *. You may take additional amounts of items in column 1, Table 8, but nothing else should be eaten or drunk.

for a day. If slimming is required cut out daily sugar, breakfast jam, half the portions of vegetables from column 2 at lunch, substitute 4 oz fresh fruit for bread and cheese at supper, cut out daily alcoholic drink. This will give a daily 1,300 Calorie diet. Artificial sweeteners containing saccharine and/or cyclamate may be taken as desired. Complete elimination of sugar is usually one of the first steps in weight reduction. Stricter reduction should not be undertaken for a long time without medical advice.

Eating between meals has raised controversy. The sensible answer seems to be that it depends on what you eat. Prolonged attempts to fight down a feeling of hunger will only lead to irritation, frustration and eventual abandonment of the diet. If you get hungry before your next meal is due it is wise to take something rather than suffer – usually it will not be in silence! What you take should be something from the low Calorie Column 1 of Table 8. What you *must not* do is eat bread, biscuits, nuts, chocolate, sweets, cakes or other moderate or high Calorie food.

These diets will not cause any dramatic loss of weight. They are designed as a different pattern for your way of eating. They will cause a slow steady loss of weight of about $\frac{1}{2}$–2 lb/week. A slow steady maintained loss of weight like this is just as good, probably better, than a dramatic fall. When a weight near the desirable (Tables 2 and 3) is reached, the diet can be liberalized gently. If the basic principle of avoiding large amounts of high Calorie foods is remembered, weight will then not be regained. As you become familiar with the diet and your weight starts falling you will find it possible to make alterations to allow for personal cravings. For instance an ounce of chocolate or sweets or 2 oz of smoked salmon could be substituted for the daily sugar ration and the lunch-time helping of potatoes.

As a further guide Table 10 gives average Calorie consumption for men and women of different size and activity. These are average figures and a certain amount of individual variation will occur. However, most people will lose weight on a diet which regularly supplies 10 per cent less Calories than the estimated amount. A diet supplying 600 Calories a day less than the number that are used will, on average, lead to a weight loss of a pound a week or just over.

TABLE 10

AVERAGE CALORIE EXPENDITURE PER 24 HOURS

Size	Sedentary	Activity Average	Very active
SMALL Men 5 ft. 6 in. or less	2,350	2,600	3,000
Women 5 ft. 2 in. or less	1,600	1,800	2,000
AVERAGE Men 5 ft. 7 in.–5 ft. 10 in.	2,600	2,900	3,300
Women 5 ft. 3 in.–5 ft. 6 in.	1,750	2,000	2,200
TALL Men 5 ft. 11 in. or more	2,850	3,200	3,600
Women 5 ft. 7 in. or more	1,950	2,200	2,400

In all groups those under 30 years old will have slightly higher and those over 50 slightly lower expenditures.

Water deprivation or excessive sweating (Turkish baths) leads to loss in weight but not loss of fat. Next time you drink the weight promptly goes on again. This is thus a quite useless way of losing weight; if carried to excess it may even be harmful.

Iron

It has been estimated that 1 in 5 women of childbearing age in this country have some degree of iron deficiency anaemia.

TABLE 11

IRON REQUIREMENTS BY AGE AND SEX

		Mg. of iron/day
Children	9–18 years	15
Men	all ages	10
Women	18–54 years	15
Women	55 plus years	10
Women	pregnant or breast feeding	20

Much of this is unrecognized and leads to a considerable amount of minor ill health, older women and men have lesser amounts of iron deficiency but still quite a considerable number are affected. The average daily requirements of iron are given in Table 11. This makes it quite clear why women are more prone to anaemia than men.

Foods that are particularly rich in iron include meat products, particularly liver and heart, yeast, wheat germ, rice bran and egg yolks. The actual intake of an adequate amount of iron is seldom a problem, the trouble is that only a small percentage is absorbed so that much of the eaten iron is wasted.

The absorption of iron may be affected by other diseases, particularly by disease of the stomach or small bowel, or by diet. Iron pills usually correct this sort of anaemia without difficulty. They are often taken routinely by pregnant mothers to prevent the onset of anaemia. They should only be taken on medical advice.

Calcium, Phosphate and Vitamin D

These three substances interact together and are responsible for the maintenance and growth of bones and teeth. Nowadays lack of one of these substances is not a problem, though in the past ricketts (due to lack of Calcium and/or vitamin D) was widespread. Pregnant mothers and growing children are the group particularly at risk. They are offered supplies of cheap milk

D

(rich in these substances) by the government and should always take advantage of this offer.

Vitamins and Essential Fatty Acids

Any normal mixed diet containing reasonable amounts of fresh fruit and vegetables and meat contains adequate amounts of all vitamins and essential fatty acids. Prolonged cooking of food tends to destroy the vitamins so that a certain proportion of raw fruit and vegetables is beneficial. A high intake of vitamin C may be helpful in combating colds, flu, styes and other minor infections. This may be readily obtained from fruit or fruit juice (oranges, lemons, grapefruit – fresh or juice, blackcurrant or rose-hip juice or syrup). Pregnant and breast-feeding mothers and young children may require additional vitamins. These are provided cheaply as fish liver oils and orange juice and should be taken as recommended by the Ministry of Health. There is no need for special vitamin pills or syrups unless these have been advised by the doctor.

Minerals

These include water, sodium, potassium, magnesium, chloride, and many trace elements. The body is very good at regulating the balance of these and except in disease or unusually extreme conditions, lack or excess of these is not met with. *Iodine* is the one exception. Lack of iodine in the soil and water may lead to a swelling in the neck called a goitre due to enlargement of the thyroid gland. This is common in mountainous districts or districts a long way from the sea. In Britain it used to be common in Derbyshire and the condition was called Derbyshire neck. Most table salt contains added iodine, this is quite enough to prevent a goitre developing and for this reason iodized salt should always be used for cooking.

Summary

The only common dietary disease in this country is obesity due to excessive Calorie consumption. Slimming implies a complete change in eating habits rather than a short period of intensive dieting. The important thing to remember is to cut down drastically on Calorie-rich foods containing large amounts of fats and carbohydrate, such as bread, potatoes, sugar, confectionery, nuts and butter. At the same time a varied diet should be consumed with adequate amounts of meat, fish, eggs, milk and fresh fruit and vegetables. On this sort of reasonably balanced diet, deficiency of other essential dietary constituents is most unlikely to occur.

11 Stress and Mental Health

In an earlier chapter we looked at stress in broad biological terms and made three main points about the ideas on which our understanding or definition of stress is based.

(1) That the term was originally derived from physics and engineering where it implies an ability to withstand strain.

(2) That all living things are in a state of constant struggle with their environment. Their survival being dependent on the achievement of a reasonable state of balance. For plants and animals the struggle is with the physical environment. As far as man in developed countries is concerned, the psychosocial or interpersonal environment is more important than the physical.

(3) Given the need to achieve reasonable success, or to live a balanced life, there is likely to be a price to pay for failure. We suggested that the defence mechanisms against too much stress took the form of a *disease reaction* which meant that the individual was opting out – by being ill – of the stress situation. We did, however, make it clear that this was a psychological or subconscious reaction. The disease or the symptoms being genuine and real. This is known as psychosomatic reaction and is the basis of what is called stress disease.

We need now to look in more detail at some of the factors which can make for success or failure in dealing with stress. Just as presymptomatic diagnosis, and knowing about the nature of one's illness is a help in dealing with it, so is an understanding of the basis of one's reaction to situations, a help in dealing with stress. The psychiatrists call this insight and it is a very valuable asset. But before looking at this it is necessary to emphasize one last basic point about stress. Inevitably because of the way in which we use the word, it gets used entirely to call attention to the harmful effects of stress. Thus 'he is stressed' or 'migraine is a stress disease'. This is fair and necessary, but what tends to be forgotten and misunderstood is that, as we have said all through, a degree of stress or challenge is essential.

This means that the right amount of stress is a good thing; it is only too much that is harmful. It means, too, that individuals have got to live with stress and anxiety without, as it were, curling up at the edges like a dried sandwich.

In this context one must make it clear that individuals vary infinitely in their ability to stand up to life. There is no panacea in understanding, that will make bricks without straw. A feeble person is likely to remain feeble, the highly strung will remain tense and the tough are unlikely ever to become sensitive. But the more they understand about the mechanisms that underlie their reactions, the better they will be able to deal with them.

Psychiatrists tend to divide acquired mental disease (in adults) into two main groups: the psychotic and the neurotic. Psychotic mental disease is regarded as serious and incapacitating. It often requires long-term hospitalization because the individual is neither responsible for, nor able to control his actions. Common conditions here are schizophrenia (split mind) and severe melancholia. Further discussion of this group of serious diseases is outside our scope, except to mention that very considerable progress has recently been made in finding methods of treating them by drugs, electric shock therapy and surgery.

Neurotic behaviour, the abnormal reaction to outside events, like an inability to go into crowds or small spaces or loss of voice before making a speech, is a mental or nervous reaction to environment demands. Because the reaction (which is as we have said, an opting out or defence mechanism) is behavioural or psychic it is called a mental disease, and comes within the psychiatrist's province.

Other disease, like headaches, indigestion, skin rashes and so on, produces, physical, bodily or somatic symptoms and have traditionally and quite reasonably been treated by the general physicians and surgeons. Until very recently, i.e. the last ten years or so, they have been content to deal purely with the symptoms, and indeed with the help of modern drugs and surgical techniques, they have been very clever at doing so. Their very success has tended to blind them to the need to look for deeper causes of the complaints. Very often symptomatic cure is adequate, but sometimes, as is shown by the following case, it is disastrous.

Some years ago the writer was asked to see a man who was aged about 50 and who worked as sales manager for a printing firm, his work involved a lot of driving and irregular meals, etc. Two weeks before he was seen he had collapsed in his car and felt generally miserable with abdominal pain and discomfort.

Two years earlier he had developed a duodenal ulcer, which was treated medically and then by operation because of two serious haemorrhages. Following the operation his company had sent him and his wife on a cruise. This produced some relief, but when seen he was obviously far from well and had a very disordered digestive system.

Before two years ago he was perfectly well. On strictly symptomatic grounds the operation was certainly justified – yet it had failed to do him any good. The reason for this failure was as follows:

This man had married early and gone into the army during the war. While he was away his wife had left him and at the end of the war he obtained a divorce. He was upset by this, but the main blow was to his pride – that his wife should leave him.

He then settled down to live with his mother who looked after him well and carefully, indeed he was probably spoilt. Very occasionally he would 'go out with a girl' and when he did he found that his sexual powers were limited.

Ten years or so later his secretary, who had worked for him for a long time, persuaded him to marry her. But when they were married he found that he was impotent and she was, not unnaturally, disappointed. Hence the digestive upset which was not helped much by operation.

This case illustrates two points about stress or neurotic disease, the first is that in this type of situation one must look for, and try to deal with, the underlying cause of the upset. The second point is a new and important one which we have not yet made; it is that in the present state of our knowledge we know very little about what causes a given person to get the psychosomatic reaction that he does.

The case we have just related might equally well have developed an acute anxiety state, which would have been a pure neurotic or psychic reaction. Equally he might have developed a skin reaction, blinding headaches or perhaps even a coronary. This has a vital implication for our understanding of psychosomatic disease and is based on the personality environment situation described earlier.

It means that if one is to get beyond the symptoms and to find out what causes them, the important thing is not *what* is wrong with this patient, but *why* is he or she ill at all. Symptoms can, as we have said, be relieved, but real cure can only come from a realization of the underlying situation. This is why psychosomatic medicine has suddenly become so extremely important. If most illness is an 'opting out or escape' mechanism, doctors must reorientate their thinking about the chain of cause and effect. It does not mean that there will be no place for drugs or surgery, but that greater understanding of the human situation will make them even more effective than they are at present.

Dr Michael Balint whose brilliant pioneering has done more than any other single doctor to develop this work in Britain relates another typical and revealing case.

He was asked to see a girl of about 14 who had recently

developed severe asthma which did not respond very well to drugs. The situation as he uncovered it was as follows: The girl was bright and had achieved a grammar school place; she did not want this at all, she wanted to stay with her friends at the secondary modern school. Her mother was ambitous for her and insisted on the grammar school. Mother also went out to work and had quite a responsible job.

By developing asthma the girl – subconsciously – achieved two ends: she was kept away from school and mother had to stay away from work to look after her.

This case illustrates another point of principle which is that the diseases of children are very often a reflection of the environmental pressures at home. Had this case gone on as in the ordinary way the child might have become a life-long asthmatic and the chain of cause and effect would have been deeply buried in her adult behaviour pattern.

What the psychiatrist can do and this is his special skill, is to find out the motivation of people's behaviour pattern and by explaining it to them, i.e. by developing insight, help them to come to terms with and deal with it.

Freud taught that the well springs of behaviour may lie deep in the subconscious mind and be based on happenings and relationships very early in life. He personally thought that sexual relationships and imagery were the critical ones, but not everyone would agree now with his emphasis on this aspect. His major contribution was to make it clear that one had to dig down and reveal the underlying cause. This is the basis of psycho-analysis. In his hands it took a very long time because the 'search' depended on discussion and what is called free association. It also depended on the patient's willingness to face facts – something that he or she was often unable to do.

What are called ab-reactive or truth drugs will speed up this process. Simpler stress reactions can be much more simply dealt with by short-term discussion, to develop insight.

It is a tragedy that, until very recently, psychiatrists, by emphasizing the sexual approach and by taking so long over their treatment, have got themselves a bad reputation. This has been coupled with the fact that mental disease which conjures up an image of jibbering maniacs in a lunatic asylum, is far from respectable. Once it is widely realized that not only is there a spectrum of mental disease from the severe and possibly incurable to the trivial, but also that most disease has a psychosomatic basis, the psychiatrist will have his rightful and useful place in the medical hierarchy.

It should be no more shaming to go to a psychiatrist than to a skin specialist. Indeed all doctors will become in large measure psychiatrists, using their skills to understand behaviour.

Mental health is in fact the major problem that faces us today. Much of the growing sickness rate which bedevils our national productivity and costs the 'health' service millions, is due to stress and poor motivation. People also do not realize that 45 per cent of the hospital beds in this country are for mental disease. Fig. 13 shows the incidence of stress in our own experience.

If then this is, in over-simplified form, the medical basis of stress disease, what help can we give the ordinary person, to cope with it. Help depends largely on understanding what is involved and we can usefully look at this a little more deeply in two respects.

The first is the need for outside interests or sources of satisfaction. One of the commonest self-delusions is that one can function in segments, i.e. one's office self is a different animal from one's domestic self. This is of course quite untrue as the individual functions in terms of his total personality and his whole environment. Thus the nagging mother-in-law or the crying baby affect performance in the office and similarly the bad-tempered boss or financial anxiety about the firm's balance sheet or the state of one's job, inevitably influence how one feels

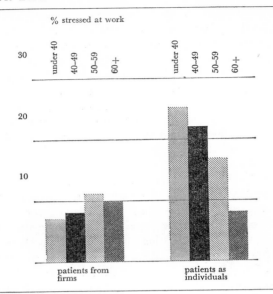

% stressed at work

Fig. 13. Incidence of stress in relation to age and patients who came as individuals or from their firms. Source: I.O.D. Medical Centre.

on arriving home. If the majority of a man's satisfactions come from work he is obviously more vulnerable than if he can boost his morale by getting real fun out of doing other things. Similarly, the housewife whose whole activity is domestic is even more vulnerable, especially when the family grows up. This is why stress diseases are so relatively common in middle-aged women.

This means that people who lead balanced lives and have relaxational pursuits which really engage their attention are less likely to succumb to stress. Clearly this becomes more important as people get older because retirement without either activity or identity may be disastrous.

The second point is to know how to minimize the sources of

stress to which one is exposed. From what we have said it is the unsolved problem that is stressful. Once the source of anxiety or frustration has been identified, it can begin to be dealt with. In trying to help stressed and worried people it is surprising how seldom they have managed to identify the source of their trouble, or if they have, they fail to take appropriate action. This involves objectively analysing the alternative courses of action that are available and then getting on and doing something about it. Having made this analysis it may be, and often is apparent, that the *status quo* is less undesirable than the alternatives. But a decision to accept the *status quo* more or less happily is in practice a stress relieving solution. It is the man who rattles 'his chips of frustration' on his shoulder, who is stressed and ill, similarly the person with a grievance who is always moaning about how hard life has treated him, is stressed.

The cheerful mortal who enjoys life and gets satisfaction out of doing his job to the best of his ability tends not to be ill.

A corollary of this approach to living sensibly is to set oneself targets that are reasonably within reach. It is no good being over-ambitious and becoming bitter over failure. Equally it is silly to be too easily satisfied. This means too that work and community activities must be organized so that there are identifiable end products to activity.

This may be difficult in a vast organization which is inevitably bureaucratic but gives security and a pension. Here one often finds that many of the people tolerate working for their living and enjoy what they do outside. The man who wants the excitement and insecurity of a smaller organization lives for his work and enjoys every minute of it. In life, like racing, there are horses for courses and it is a help to get on to the right track.

There are two last practical points about dealing with stress, particularly for busy people. The first is to realize that the busier one is, the more important it is to get one's priorities right, so that one's available time and energy can be deployed with the best tactical expediency. This may involve admitting that for the time being there are certain problems that must be put on one side. It also means not wasting too much time on the easy and trivial problems. Although this does apply more to busy people, it is equally true of ordinary life. How often does one hear one's friends and neighbours literally tearing themselves to shreds, either over the most trivial things, or matters that they cannot hope to influence.

The second is that in terms of inter-personal relationships, either in the small unit of the family, or the larger unit of work, individuals ought to give much more consideration to the effects that their decisions, reactions and actions will have on others. Stress is caused either by thoughtlessness or unreasonable dominance. A tough supervisor or an irrascible boss, can when he is in a bad temper, send ripples through an organization which cause an unbelievable amount of stress, anxiety and reduced productivity. Very often the individuals concerned are not aware of the chaos they cause, and the same is true of families; someone should tell them.

Losing one's temper or snapping back irritably and irrationally is probably the commonest single stress symptom. It reflects the inability of the person concerned to deal rationally with the situation, so he opts out by explosion. It is his own inadequacy rather than the competence of his associates, that is really in question.

It is, however, much better to reveal one's aggression or disapproval than it is to harbour grievances and go round muttering with discontent. But clearly there are ways and ways of doing this. Most people respect honest speaking and resent well-meaning hypocrisy.

Fatigue is often mistaken for stress – it is in fact a quite different and equally complicated entity, the details of which we cannot go into here. Fatigue is the natural concomitant of work and living a full life. It is more a reflection of mood than it is of physical state, although sheer physical exhaustion can and does occur.

A tired man can either be discouraged by failure or encouraged by success or a new stimulus. A tired man is thus likely to have a lower stress threshold than a fit person. This is why it is so important to keep life in balance and to avoid undue fatigue. When one is over-tired minor stress complaints are more likely, for instance, insomnia, indigestion or irritability. Delusions of indespensability are a common end result of stress and fatigue – too busy for a holiday.

The point here is to know our own devils and having got to know them, to regard them as a friendly warning rather than an awful curse. Thus if one knows the chain of cause and effect which produces stress symptoms they can often be easily recognized and dealt with. In stable, well-integrated people they are, as we have just said, to be regarded as a 'useful devil'. If they are more deeply rooted in subconscious behaviour the help of a psychiatrist may be required to dig them out. Good psychiatrists are few and far between, but they can be worth their weight in gold.

Mental health is easy to consider but difficult to define. It is intimately related, as we have said, to what is traditionally called physical well-being. But it is also a reflection of man's relation to man and as such cannot be separated from the way in which the community is run and indeed to the way in which one community relates to another.

That we live in troubled and tortuous times is apparent to all, this is reflected in a growing toll of physical and mental disease. At this moment in our evolution it is quite clear that we have largely failed to live sensibly in the world which we have created. Unless we get rapidly better at this, at all levels, work, home, nationally and internationally, the future is too awful to contemplate.

There is little doubt however that the quality of our

existence both in the home and in the factory or office currently leaves much to be desired. If we are to minimize stress and make it possible for each of us to give of his best, leadership and motivation must be entirely reorganized so that reasonable people can be seen to achieve reasonable targets.

Our current state of relative disease is due to the failure of many of us to balance our personality environment equations. It is obvious that the over-security of the welfare state is only a very partial answer.

12 Physical Fitness

In discussing the problems of maintaining reasonable health and minimizing the chances of cardiovascular disease in the main part of this book, the need for regular physical exercise has already been stressed. Reference was also made to the benefits this may have in both protecting against and reducing the effects of a coronary thrombosis. Emphasis was also laid on the fact that it is generally easier for thinnish people to remain active than it is for the overweight and sluggish.

Fitness is as much an attitude of mind as a physical state, although some aspects of the latter can be measured objectively, as we shall see in this section. Unfortunately it is virtually impossible either to measure well-being, or to calculate the effect that this may have on efficiency and productivity. But one can make a fair generalization that a fit man is likely to stand up better to the stresses and strains of a demanding life than a sluggish man.

Regular exercise can be expected to do three things, improve endurance, mobility and strength. Joints are likely to give better service if they are regularly put through their full range of movements and muscle strength can only be maintained by use.

There is really no age limit for regular exercise provided there are no physical limitations. Indeed it is vital that people should, as they get older, go out of their way to keep active. Agricultural workers, for instance, can go on doing heavy work for years because they are doing it all the time. In this way, too, strength is kept up.

Changes in the pulse rate resulting from physical activity can be used as a rough measure of cardiovascular fitness. We have seen that when the muscles require a higher blood supply to cope with the desired activity, it is essential that the pulse and respiration rate should go up. Also what is called the stroke volume of the heart increases. That is, it pumps out a larger volume of blood per beat. If it does this efficiently it is likely to have a larger stroke volume at rest and can thus meet the resting demand with a lower pulse rate. This is why athletes tend to have slow pulses when at rest.

The degree to which activity will raise the pulse depends on:

1. The number and size of muscles involved.
2. The work load, perhaps in terms of repetitions or resistance.
3. Pauses in the work.

Pulse rate at the end of the work is called the *work pulse*. Clearly the recovery rate can be measured by counting it again after a given time – say 90 seconds. This is called the *active* pause.

Thus if the work pulse is 160 per minute and 90 seconds later it is 140 per minute. The difference is 20 beats per minute.

If this difference is expressed as a fraction of the work pulse it can be used as a recovery index. Thus in our example it would be $\frac{20}{160} = \frac{1}{8}$

We know that a recovery rate of $\frac{1}{8}$ is poor, $\frac{1}{4}$ fair, $\frac{1}{3}$ good, and less than this very good.

Types of exercise

There is no one ideal method of achieving fitness: any exercise is better than none, but to be really effective the following 'four Rs' should be embraced:

1. *Range* of movement, which must be complete to ensure that all joints and muscles are exercised.
2. *Repetition*: exercises consist of repeated movements and the number of repetitions must gradually increase to produce a systematic improvement in the heart and lungs.

3. *Resistance* to the muscles should be progressively increased as the muscles themselves gain strength.

4. *Recreation* is important and the most attractive method of exercising should be adopted if possible so that interest is maintained.

Sports and games like golf, tennis and badminton can be played well into late life, but if this is done it must be regular and at least once a week. Even for the middle-aged there is nothing more dangerous than the annual parents' match. Coaches know, however, that if stiffness is to be avoided muscles should be used against resistance about twice a week. It must also be remembered that individual games only use certain muscles, so that the regular tennis player will feel stiff after a round of golf – and vice versa. This is an argument in favour of a regular and planned system of exercises such as I am outlining in this section. Obviously, too, one must get back to activity gradually after a lay-off.

Free standing exercise

There are in practice a number of forms of taking exercise or using the muscles. The best known is called *free exercise* as personified by the traditional P.T. which we all did at school and in the army, and as many women do at Keep Fit classes. P.T. is easy to do, is flexible enough to meet all needs and requires no apparatus. It does, however, seem to be difficult to keep people motivated to do it regularly.

The Canadian Air Force 5BX Plan, published as a Penguin, is the best known example of this type of activity.

Isometric exercise

The word Isometric means that the muscle or muscles are contracted to hold a fixed or static position irrespective of the resistance.

113

Holding one's arm sideways means that the shoulder group of muscles are working isometrically to hold this position.

Extreme examples of this are when you attempt to move an immovable object such as pushing against a wall or trying to uproot a tree.

They have in fact been used since classical times and have a respectable lineage. They certainly make muscles work and they also put up blood pressure, perhaps in fact more so than brisk active movement.

Opinions vary about their value as a training procedure, but they certainly have a place in this field, and there is no doubt that isometrics increase strength but not mobility. They can, of course, be combined with free standing exercises to give a useful schedule. Individuals with a raised blood pressure should only indulge in isometrics under skilled supervision.

Weight training

Weight training has become accepted in almost every area of physical activity, from the sports field to hospital rehabilitation. In my view weight training is the best form of all-round exercise.

Weight training is not synonymous with heavy weight lifting. It is basically free exercise in which the muscles work against the additional resistance of weights and the latter can be varied to suit the individual's requirements. Even a golfer or a cricketer is indulging in weight training of some sort. A golf club and a cricket bat are light weights. Weight training makes use of dumb-bells or an adjustable, disc-loading bar-bell. To begin with resistance is usually very light so that movements can be learned comfortably, well within the capabilities of the exerciser. Weights can be added or increased as the individual requires them and so an estimate of his or her progress is easily made. Such motivation is one of the reasons why weight training is so good a form of exercising.

Fig. 14. A typical dumb-bell and bar-bell. For home use fewer detachable weights would be needed by most individuals (see details of weights recommended in weight training exercise schedules).

Equipment

A modern disc-loading bar-bell set consists of the following basic components (a) the bar-bell rod or bar, 1 in in diameter and ranging from 4 ft to 7 ft in length, (b) the bar-bell sleeve, a chromium-plated steel tube, 3–4 ft long, which slips over the central section of the bar-bell rod, (c) the discs – round, flat, metal plates weighing from $\frac{1}{2}$ lb to 50 lb as a rule, and sliding on to the bar-bell rod, (d) collar – rings of metal with fixing screws which are put on to the rod after the weights in order to keep them safely in position during exercise. The dumb-bell set is very similar except that the rod is only 12–18 in long and the sleeve or dumb-bell grip is only about 5 in long. Some dumb-bells consist only of one piece of moulded metal and may be preferred for home use.

115

The benefits of weight training

For every free exercise there is a corresponding exercise with weights. Each joint and the associated muscles can similarly be exercised over their complete range but with better results since they are working against a resistance. Visible improvements in physique are apparent after five or six weeks. Similarly cardiovascular efficiency, strength, and joint and muscle ability will have improved noticeably.

A numerical assessment of the improvement can be made by multiplying the weight by the number of repetitions performed in a given time. For example, if you perform six exercises with a 10-lb bar-bell and carry out 10 repetitions of each exercise, you perform 60 movements of 10 lb, or 600 work units. When in poor physical condition, as at the beginning of a course, you may, with rest periods between each exercise, take 20 minutes to complete the six exercises. As your condition improves you will be able to increase the weight and the number of repetitions. Similarly rest pauses will be reduced.

The adjustability of weight training makes it suitable for individuals of any age, or sex, or physical condition, except where certain organic diseases preclude it. Weights can be set to suit the individual and the size and strength of the muscles (or groups of muscles) involved. Should an exercise be prescribed for the upper arm muscles, the load will naturally be lighter than that for the combined power of the legs and back.

It was mentioned previously that cardiovascular efficiency is improved as a result of weight-training exercises. Often this is disputed; probably because the disputers equate weight training with competitive weight lifting. Of course, the raising of heavy weights, such as those used by the professional weight lifter, will not raise the pulse rate or rate of breathing noticeably, but by lifting light weights repeatedly and vigorously the pulse rate and breathing rate must be raised which will lead to improvements in the output of the circulatory and respiratory systems. Excellent result have been obtained through performing five basic exercises, beginning with 10 repetitions and working up to 20 or 30. Anyone who wishes to build up greater endurance should step up the number of repetitions to 50 or even 100.

Although weight-training programmes vary in respect of the exercises performed and the weights used, to progress in a programme the following basic points will apply.

(a) to raise the pulse rate and depth and frequency of breathing, increase the number of repetitions of each exercise and reduce or cut out the rest pauses between them. The duration of rest pauses must depend upon the pulse recovery rate.

(b) to develop speed and power increase the speed of the actual movement.

(c) to develop strength, power, speed, and muscular development increase the resistance, either by increasing the weight or by altering the starting position so that leverage is made more difficult for the specific muscles involved.

(The schedules suggested give details.)

We can summarize the advantages of weight training as follows:

(1) It is a great time saver. Two or three exercise periods each week, each period lasting 15–30 minutes, can produce excellent results. The extra resistance provided by the weight allows a smaller number of repetitions than in free-standing exercise.

(2) When the exerciser is extremely busy and can spend only a few minutes exercising, two or three special 'massive' exercises can be selected. These are exercises involving large muscle groups, such as those of the trunk, and they produce a demand on the heart and lungs as well as providing major joints and muscles with exercise.

(3) The resistance can be adapted to suit age, sex, and

physical condition and this means that, should the exerciser be forced to stop for a period, he merely reduces the weights a little until he gets back to his former condition.

(4) Progress can be measured very easily by recording the weight used, the number of repetitions, and the time required to complete each exercise period.

(5) Above all, those of us with qualifications and experience in a wide field of physical activity believe that the satisfaction and feeling of well-being derived from a progressive and systematic weight-training programme is well worthwhile.

13 Exercise Programmes

Before outlining a suggested exercise schedule it is worthwhile providing some advice on two points which often cause concern – breathing during exercises and suitable clothing.

Breathing

As a general rule you should breathe in as a weight (that of the body itself or any additional weight) is being raised, and out as it is lowered. Similarly, breathe in when the spine is being extended and out when it is flexed. This is quite natural since the size of the rib-cage increases when the spine is extended. Occasionally these two actions conflict. For example during an abdominal sit-up, as the exerciser raises his head and body from the floor to a sitting position, the spine is being flexed. He should, therefore, breathe out when sitting up and in when returning to the prone position.

It is inadvisable to hold one's breath while exercising – always try to breathe freely – and it is equally bad to force one's breathing. The severity of the exercise will automatically produce the necessary demand for oxygen. If possible the exerciser should try to breathe in and out through his or her nose, but the ability to do this will depend on the individual and when excessive demands for oxygen are made during vigorous exercise breathing through the mouth will almost certainly be necessary.

Some movements seem to defy any sort of rhythmical breathing. It is then advisable to breathe as freely and comfortably as possible without trying to impose any rhythm.

Clothing

Some people automatically think of shorts, singlets, and gym shoes whenever they think of exercise. It is most important, however, that the body is covered adequately during chilly conditions so that it isn't working to make up for heat loss as well as providing the energy for exercise. A track suit or similar clothing is ideal in such conditions. Whatever you choose to wear it is vital that freedom of movement is permitted. As you exercise it may be necessary to remove some clothing but do ensure that the body does not cool down too much before taking a shower or bath afterwards.

Suggested exercise schedules for men

Free standing schedule No. 1

Part 1. Exercises for mobility

The first aim of those about to begin exercise is to mobilize all the major joints of the body; fitness and strength training can be introduced in the correct amount at a later date.

This mobility helps to prevent over-stretching and minor strains. As the exerciser progresses, it is necessary to have a fair degree of general mobility, so that the starting positions may be assumed in comfort.

The following system is simple, yet it provides the requirements in mind. One repetition is the movement from the starting position through the whole action and back to the original starting position.

120

1. Arm circling

Feet astride, arms circling
forwards, upwards and
backwards. Keep the arms
close to the head and hips
during the movement.
Progress from 10
repetitions to 25.

2. Trunk bending

Feet astride, hands on hips,
trunk bending from side
to side, keeping the body
plane vertical.
Progress from 10
repetitions to 25.

3. Knee raising

Feet together, hands on
hips, alternate knee
raising to chest.
Progress from 10
repetitions to 25.

121

4. Trunk rotation

Feet astride, arms bent,
elbows shoulder level,
finger-tips touching in
front of upper chest. Keep
the hips and legs still,
rotate the head, trunk and
arms, at the same time
stretch and swing the arm
corresponding to the side
to which the trunk is being
turned; continue in a nice
even rhythmical manner.
Progress from 10
repetitions to 25.

5. Half knee bends

Stand on toes, heels
together, hands on hips;
knee half bends.
Progress from 10
repetitions to 25.

6. Back lying, knee raising

Lie on back and raise
alternate thighs on to
chest.
Progress from 10
repetitions to 25.

At this stage I would like to point out that there are many far more interesting movements than those listed, but they are progressions, and often require a considerable amount of skill and co-ordination of movement. We must be realistic; when movements are so complex that a teacher is required, then they are not suitable for home training in the early stages.

Part 1 of this Schedule should be carried out every second day for the first week or two, then six days each week, for four to six weeks. Mobilizing exercises should always be carried out at an easy rhythm, without jerking or over-stretching.

Free standing schedule No. 1

Part 2. Exercises for strength

This part of Schedule 1 should be continued for eight to ten weeks. Continue with Part 1 to loosen up before carrying out the Part 2 exercises which give strength to the major muscles.

1a. Table press-ups
Arms, shoulders, chest

Body straight and at an angle of 45° hands resting on a table or piece of furniture of similar height. Push with hands to raise body. If the movement is still too difficult, use a higher object. Progress from 4 repetitions to 12.

2a. Back arching
Back

Lie face down, hands on
hips. Raise head and
shoulders, holding raised
position for one second.
Progress from 8
repetitions to 20.

3a. Step-ups
Leg and breathing

Step on and off chair or
stool. Counts should be
taken on the first leg to
move.
Progress from 10
repetitions to 20.

4a. Sit-ups
Waist-line

Lie on back with knees
slightly bent and feet held
down. Now sit up; swing
arms to assist the raising
of the trunk.
Progress from 8
repetitions to 12.

Free standing schedule No. 2

The exerciser should now have reached a condition of fitness which permits this all-purpose schedule to be carried out. Should time be a problem, leave out a few movements, those which call mainly for muscle strength.

This schedule need not be performed daily; this can be too demanding for the average person. Executed correctly two or three times weekly, this schedule will produce excellent results.

1. Arms circling

As in Schedule 1, but trunk inclined at an angle of 45°, back flat and kept still.
Progress from 10 repetitions to 20.

2. Side bends

Feet astride, hands clasped on head, count to the side from which the movement started.
Progress from 10 repetitions to 20.

125

3. Running on the spot

Raise knees high, count on
first leg to be raised.
Progress from 20
repetitions to 30.
Keep even running tempo.

4. Inclined trunk rotating

As exercise 4 in Schedule
1, Part 1, but trunk
inclined forward to 45°,
count on first arm to move.
Progress from 10
repetitions to 20.

The Principles of progression in free standing fitness and strength work

Increase in the volume of work in free standing exercises for improved cardiovascular efficiency is achieved quite simply by increasing the number of repetitions, increasing the tempo of the exercise, and reducing the rest pauses between exercises or sets of repetitions.

To step up the intensity of work for strength building by free standing exercises is a more difficult problem, and I feel that in addition to the basic principles already covered earlier in the book it might be advisable to give a few examples of how we can work up to fairly strong muscular movements without using any form of apparatus.

For the first example let us take a difficult *abdominal movement* – sitting up *on an abdominal board.*

The board can be at any angle, with the feet at the high end, and the exerciser is required to sit up until the trunk is vertical. When the board is near to or steeper than 45° a fair degree of abdominal power is required to perform even a few repetitions. Many stout business people will find sit-ups on the floor too difficult, let alone sit-ups at such a steep angle.

So let us deal with those very weak abdominal muscles and the theory behind the method.

The board should be placed at an angle of more than 45°, the exerciser should lie face upwards, head at the high end; this places the trunk in a starting position, which would in fact only be half up towards the sitting position if he lay flat on the floor. The exerciser will therefore find it reasonably easy to sit up from this inclined position. To progress, he adds repetitions as before until he reaches 10 or 20. Then he lowers or reduces the angle of the board. He continues in this manner, performing 10–20 repetitions, until the board is fully lowered to a horizontal position.

When 10–20 movements are possible in this position, the board is again raised to an angle of 15°–20°. But this time the feet are at the high end. Progress as before, reversing the angle of the board when 10–20 repetitions are possible at each stage. It is possible to develop abdominal strength so that the board can be well on its way to an angle approaching the vertical, even in middle age, although this, of course, is far from necessary in the pursuit of middle age fitness.

The same principles apply to those who find it impossible to do a single press-up from the floor. This is a popular movement where the palms of the hands are placed under the shoulders and about eighteen inches apart. The body is then held rigid and raised clear off the floor by extending the arms until they are straight. The body is supported throughout by the hands and feet.

Those individuals unable to perform such a movement take up a similar position as on the floor, except that the hands are placed on an object about chest-high such as a chest of drawers. The feet, of course, remain on the floor and the body is straight, whilst the arms are bent and straightened as before. Gradually the muscles will respond and the movement will become easier; it is then time to lower the angle of the body by placing the hands on an object about waist-high (e.g. a table). Soon the exerciser will find that press-ups on the floor no longer present a problem.

You can now reverse the procedure by placing the toes on the seat of a chair, and the hands and chest on the floor. Keep your body straight and, as you extend your arms, a great deal of the body weight will be on your arms.

Leg strength

We can now complete this short chapter with the development of leg power, once more applying the basic principle of positioning the body to provide the muscles with slight resistance at first and then, as the muscle groups improve in power, taking up a new position to throw greater resistance on the specific muscles involved. The resistance may also be reversed by applying greater speed to the contraction of the muscles, as in leaping. A glance at Rudolf Nureyev's tremendously powerful legs should prove this point. But it is extremely unlikely that any reader will be enthusiastic about a ballet routine, so we will return to something less intricate in technique. I refer to the *one leg full squat*, a fair feat of strength and much too strenuous for most. Nevertheless, this movement will be our aim in leg strength in order to bring out the principles of progression for the legs.

In this exercise you are required to take one foot off the floor, and lower the whole body bending the supporting leg until you are in a full-legged squat, with the other leg held out in front and clear of the floor.

This is not attainable for the majority of people, but here is how you would progress towards the accomplishment of this feat. Place the left foot on a small, but solid stool, take the weight on the other leg, and steadily extend the left leg. Perform this ten times with each leg, giving little or no assistance from the other leg.

As the legs improve in strength, the height of the stool or object is increased to near table height, by this time you will be nearly ready to do the final movement as first described on the floor level.

Please do not think for one moment that I recommend those three very advanced free exercises for strength building, I merely wish to point out the vast difference between exercise and endurance, between fitness or cardiovascular efficiency and strength-building.

Exercising with weights

The first thing to learn is the correct lifting position from the floor, which will be referred to simply as the *lifting position*.

Assume the lifting position as follows: insteps under the bar; feet hip width apart; knees bent to 90°; back flat, but not vertical; hands gripping the bar; knuckles to the front; arms straight; shoulders a little in advance of the bar; eyes looking forwards.

Whenever lifting a bar from the floor to the thighs, or higher, observe the following points: as soon as you are ready to make the first effort, you must aim to raise the head, shoulders and hips at the same time, this will cause the knees to move backwards as the legs are extended, allowing the bar to be lifted almost vertically upwards from its original position on the floor.

As the bar accelerates and passes the knees, swing the thighs towards the bar. If the bar is to be brought to the chest, the elbows must then be bent to point sideways as the bar passes the waist. The elbows are whipped forwards and under the bar to support it as it comes to rest across the top of the chest and shoulders.

Once you have studied, and mastered the above movements you will find that all the other exercises are comparatively simple in their execution.

The above detailed guidance to lifting may seem a little complex, but I feel it is necessary, as most exercises employing weights resistance begin from the floor.

Limbering up

Assuming once more that you have progressed from a spell of free exercises and you are now ready to try your hand at weight resistance movements, you are still recommended to use a few free standing movements to stretch the muscles and joints gently over their full range of movement. This need not take more than three minutes or a dozen repetitions of four or five simple movements, such as set in Free Standing Schedule No. 1. This will loosen you and raise your pulse rate ready for your first gentle weight-training routine.

The introductory routine

No pretence is made that this schedule is complete in any way, the purpose here is principally to generate confidence in the handling of weights. The movements are few, but basic, and later they will be of great advantage to those who are really serious about their state of fitness. The recommended number of workouts is not less than two per week and not more than three. Do not exercise on two consecutive days but avoid gaps of more than two days' inactivity.

Schedule 1

Note: Bar-bell will be abbreviated to B/B and Dumb–bell to D/B.

1. Clean to chest

Assume lifting position,
lift B/B from floor on to
chest.
Weight 15/25 lb. Progress
from 8 repetitions to 15.

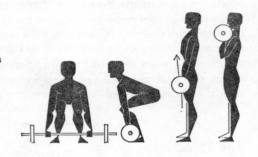

2. Press from behind neck

The B/B is pressed from
behind the neck to arm's
length overhead.
Bar only 15 lb. Progress
from 8 repetitions to 12.

3. Side to side bends

One D/B, feet wide apart,
free hand on hip, bend
from side to side, keep
shoulder in line with heels.
5 lb D/B. Progress from
10 repetitions to 16.

4. Half knee bends

One D/B in each hand,
heels on a 1-inch high
block or book.
Use 5 lb D/Bs. Progress
from 10 repetitions to 16.

5. Press on bench

With B/B. Back lying on
bench, bar resting on mid
chest, hands shoulder
width, press the B/B
upwards to finish on a
vertically extended arm.
Weight 20/30 lb. Progress
from 8 repetitions to 15.

6. Sit-ups

Finish with sit-ups from
lying position, hands
behind neck holding disk.

You may progress to Schedule 2 in your own time when you
decide that you are ready.

Schedule 2

1. Chin-high pull

The B/B is pulled from the
floor up to the chin, the
elbows should finish sideways at chin level.
Weight 25/30 lb. Progress
from 10 repetitions to 20.

2. Seated press from chest

Press the B/B from its
resting place on the chest
to arm's length overhead.
Weight 20/30 lb. Progress
from 8 repetitions to 12.

3. B/B curl

Grip the B/B shoulder
breadth, palms to the
front, bar resting across
the top front part of the
thighs, bend and stretch
the arms keeping the B/B
close to the body.
Weight 15/20 lb. Progress
from 8 repetitions to 12.

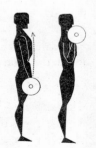

4. Side bends D/B

As before (Schedule 1) but the free hand should be behind the neck. Weight 5/10 lb. Progress from 10 repetitions to 20.

5. Squat to knee level

B/B behind neck, and resting comfortably on the shoulder, feet a little wider than hip width. Bend the knees until the thighs are in line with the floor. Weight 20/30 lb. Progress from 10 repetitions to 20.

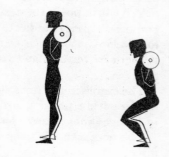

6. Wide grip bench press

As Schedule 1, but with a grip wider than shoulder width. Weight 25/30 lb. Progress from 10 repetitions to 15.

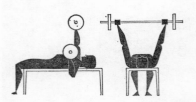

135

7. Sit-up with feet high

Use sit-up board, or whilst back lying, place heels on raised base, bed or chair, now sit up to touch the toes. No weight. Two groups of repetitions, comfortable maximum.

If you are happy with this schedule, you may continue for three months, adding gently to the weight whenever the maximum repetitions are reached. When you add weights, however, you must reduce the repetitions to the starting number, which is usually around 10 counts.

You will notice in the next schedule, No. 3, an asterisk by some exercises. This is to indicate that high repetitions should be used to develop *cardiovascular fitness*. Exercises without an asterisk are strength movements and resistance is more important in these exercises.

The exerciser who finds 20 repetitions easy to perform, and has now reached a fair standard of fitness can, if he wishes, work up to 30 repetitions on any exercise marked with an asterisk.

This does *not* apply to any exercise that has no asterisk against it.

Schedule 3.

1. High pull to arm's length*

Pull the B/B from floor to overhead.
Weight 35/40 lb. Progress from 10 repetitions to 20 or more.

2. 2 D/B overhead press

Begin with the D/Bs held at the sides of shoulders, rods facing fore and aft, press upwards to arm's length.
Weights 10/15 lb in each hand. 2 sets of 8 repetitions.

3. Close grip upright rowing

Standing, close grip, pull the bar from the thighs to the neck.
Weight 20/30 lb. 2 sets of 8 repetitions.

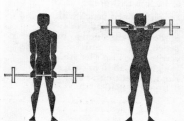

4. Side bend with D/B*

D/B held behind neck.
Weight 5/10 lb. Progress
from 10 repetitions to 16.

5. Squat

to knee level, as Schedule 2.
Weight 30/40 lb.
Repetitions: set 1, 10/13;
set 2, 10/13.

6. Incline D/B press

Lie on inclined bench with
a D/B in each hand, rods
in the same direction as the
bench, press upwards
vertically to arm's length.
Weights 10/15 lb in each
hand. Repetitions: set 1,
8/10; set 2, 8/10.

138

7. Power cleans*

Place the two D/Bs fore
and aft, stand between
them, lift them from the
floor to the shoulders,
lower to the thighs, then
to the floor and repeat.
Weights 10/15 lb in each
hand. 10/20 repetitions **or**
more.

8. Back lying, both legs raising*

If this should prove too
difficult bend the knees a
little, this reduces the
leverage.
No weight. Repetitions:
two or three groups or
sets of repetitions to
comfortable maximum.

Free standing exercises for women

1. Arm circling

Stand with feet 12″
apart, arms at
sides. Make large
circles with alternate
arms, moving arms for-
wards, upwards and
backwards keeping arms
close to head and thighs.
10–24 repetitions.

2. Knee raising

Stand with feet together,
raise alternate knees as
high as possible.
10–24 repetitions.

3. Side bending

Stand with feet wide
astride, hands at sides.
Bend sideways to the left
from waist, pushing left
hand as far down left leg
as possible, keeping body
on a vertical plane. Re-
peat to right.
10–20 repetitions.

4. Toe touching

Stand with feet 12" apart, arms at full stretch above head. Bend forward to touch floor between feet, bending knees slightly, move arms back to vertical position overhead. 10–20 repetitions.

5. Push-ups on to knee

Lie face down, legs together and straight, hands placed under shoulder. Push up on hands to arm's length keeping knees and feet on floor. Sit back on to knees then return to start position. 6–14 repetitions.

6. Chest raising

Lie face down, arms at
sides, hands under thighs.
Raise head and shoulders
as high as possible then
lower to floor.
8–16 repetitions.

7. Sit-ups and toe touching

Lie on back, arms at sides.
Raise trunk, moving arms
to touch toes with hands.
Return to start position.
8–20 repetitions.
(Use an arm swinging
movement if the above is
too difficult.)

Figure forming exercises for women using weights

1. High pull-up

Assume start position, feet apart to hip width, insteps under the bar, knees bent. Keep the back flat and the arms straight, hands grasping the bar shoulder width. Raise bar vigorously above head at arm's length and rise high on toes. Breathe in on the way up and out when returning weight to floor.

2. Seated press from chest

Start in sitting position, feet together with bar held shoulder-high against the chest, hands wide apart. Raise (press) the B/B from the chest to arm's length vertically above the shoulders. Breathe in on the upward movement and out as the bar is returned to the chest.

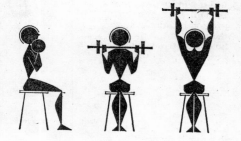

143

3. Heels raising and knees full bending

At start hold the B/B behind the head on shoulders, toes pointing out, heels together. Bend the knees fully. Breathe out on the way down and in on the way up.
Use a book or block of wood (at first) if difficulty in maintaining balance is experienced.

4. Side bend

Assume start position as illustrated. Keep the right arm straight whilst bending to the left breathing in whilst moving away from the D/B. Return to start position breathing out at the same time. Repeat holding D/B in left hand, bending to right then left.

5. Bent forward rowing

Assume position in the first diagram body at 45° to the vertical, elbows raised just above wrists. Eyes to the front. Lower the B/B until arms fully extended. This is the start position. Pull the arms up to the neck raising the elbows upwards and sideways. Breathe in on the upward movement and out on the downward movement.

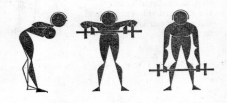

144

6. Fore and aft squats

Start position as indicated in the first diagram, left leg 30 in. or so behind right, B/B held at shoulder-height under chin. Keep near heel high off the ground. Lower the body so that right hip almost touches right heel (knee should ideally be just in front of toes). Then straighten both legs returning to start position. Breathe freely throughout.

7. Bent arm pull-over

Lie on a bench with the legs bent at the knees and with the feet resting on the floor (if no bench is available then perform the straight arm pull over below). Hold the B/B as indicated across the chest, arms bent, palms facing upwards. Move the B/B backwards over the head keeping the arms bent at right-angles and the B/B close to the head until the second position is reached. Return the B/B to the start position. Breathe in as the B/B is lowered backwards and downwards and out during the forward movement.

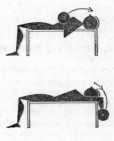

145

Alternative exercise – straight arm pull over

Lie on the floor feet slightly apart and with the bar of the B/B only resting across the tops of the thighs, arms straight (alternatively use a 2½-lb disc in each hand). Keeping the arms straight raise the bar back over the head until it reaches the floor behind the head. Breathe in as the B/B is moved back behind the head and out on the return movement.

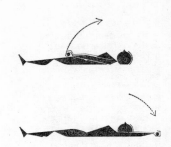

8. Back lying with arm circling

This is best done whilst lying on a bench but the floor is suitable if no bench is available. Adopt start position with the arms reaching straight to the thighs, hands together, each holding a 1½-lb disc or equivalent weights. Cross arms at wrist and raise them upwards and backwards to a position behind the head. Move arms away from each other out sideways – keeping them straight – and bringing them back to start position above thighs. Breathe in when arms held out at right-angles to body, and out when they are moving backwards from start position.

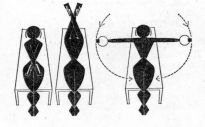

146

9. Sit-ups

(no weights)
Lie on the floor (face up) with hands clasped behind the head, feet held under a B/B or chair. Keeping hands clasped behind the head sit up to a position beyond the vertical and then lower the trunk to the floor.

This is not a book on weight training and those interested in further progression should study *Modern Weight Training* which specializes in advanced weight training.

Accent has been placed on resistive exercise in the shape of weight training, for I firmly believe that it has advantages in terms of adaptability to our three main ingredients of fitness, *mobility, cardiovascular fitness* and *muscular strength.*

However, I have no hesitation in agreeing that almost any type of systematic exercise is better than none at all.

Your selection of method depends firstly on your enthusiasm, and secondly that which is best suited to your age, condition and the time available.

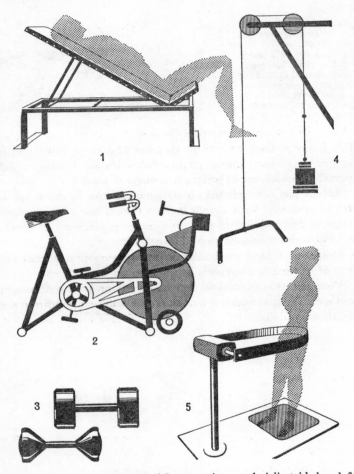

FIG. 15. Various pieces of physical fitness equipment. 1. Adjustable bench for all types of chest and backlying arm exercise. 2. Static or remedial cycle. 3. Solid dumb-bells. 4. Wall puller machine for exercising arms and back. 5. Vibrating massage belt.

Regularity of training

Most people are discouraged from exercise when they find that the pressure of business and other activities prevents them from exercising with the regularity of an Olympic athlete.

This is not necessary, by any manner or means, with one proviso: try to exercise every second day until you reach a fair degree of fitness. This may take between six and ten weeks but after this period you will be able to exercise with good results, with a lot less discipline.

Here is an average sample of a ten-week period taken at my city gym where over 70 per cent of my members are company directors and executives.

Week	1 – 2 – 3 – 4 – 5 – 6 – 7 – 8 – 9 – 10
No. of work-outs	3 – 3 – 0 – 2 – 1 – 3 – 2 – 2 – 2 – 3

This table shows excellent results. The concentrated effort of weight training is a great time saver and one of the most valuable assets.

14 Living Sensibly

Inevitably in writing a book like this one has to pay more attention to the gloomy side of the picture. To make our points we have had to outline what we think are the main medical problems which face our community and to try and point out some of the reasons which have led to our present state of ill health. We have also tried to explain the chain of cause and effect which in its turn produces the pathological changes in the body which lead to what is called organic disease. We have tried to relate these to the behaviour and reactions of the people concerned and in doing so have tried to show how the dice might be loaded in favour of prevention.

At the risk of being repetitious it is thought worth while to try and pull all this together in a final chapter on sensible living – but we do hope that readers will not feel that we are trying, like so many religious breast-beaters, to sound a clarion call for sackcloths and ashes. But many of the 'diseases' that currently afflict man in developed countries are due to overindulgence, and if prevention or mitigation is to be successful some discrimination is called for – as well as a certain amount of self-discipline.

Although we have inevitably to urge our readers to make some virtue out of the necessity for self-denial, we hope that we have made one point abundantly clear. That is that life really is for living zestfully and without grievance. It is, we have suggested, the moaning minnies, the grievance mongers and the unfulfilled who are more likely to be ill. Reasonably well-adjusted people, getting satisfaction out of what they do, are, we think, less likely to be ill. Indeed they are seldom found, unless they have pushed themselves too hard, to be seriously ill or incapacitated by chronic disease.

On the basis of what we have said, and supported to some extent by the figures quoted, the following rules for sensible living are suggested.

First – Know something about the hazards and pitfalls which may befall you. Accidents are one of the commonest causes of premature death in young men, at work, in the home and on the roads. Cardiovascular disease, which there are now good grounds for thinking may be at least partially preventable, takes its toll of the middle-aged. Chronic bronchitis and mental ill health – including stress – is a major cause of illness and disability.

Second – Diet. It is a paradox that whereas undeveloped countries suffer from serious malnutrition, in developed countries over-nutrition which is expressed as obesity is the commonest disease. Perhaps we need an anti-carbohydrate movement as a corollary to Oxfam – give your cakes, sugar, bread and potatoes to Africa might be a new battle-cry.

Overweight carries an increased mortality. It puts up blood pressure, places a greater load on bones, joints and the heart and may be reflected in higher cholesterol levels.

Weight control is, in the absence of disease, a simple matter of Calory book-keeping. If you eat more Calories than you need they are banked as fat. In the chapter on diet we included tables of average and reasonable heights for weight and age. If weight control is important it means that a pair of bathroom scales becomes an important weapon in the armoury of preventive medicine. Every house should have one.

If you want to know what it is like to lose a stone in weight, carry a 14-lb sack of sand around for a couple of days and then leave it in the garden.

But weight control does not mean a life of frugal abstinence. It means getting your weight down to bogey and then so

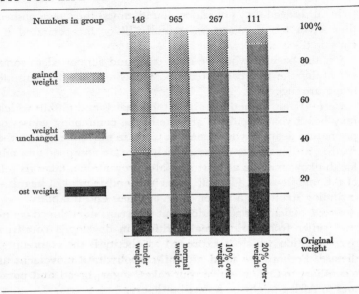

FIG. 16. Weight changes in a sample group of men followed up for at least a year. Note that overweight men can bring their weight down. Source: Institute of Directors Medical Centre.

arranging your diet so that you eat the things you like and enjoy, and make do with less of the things you like less. Eating is both a habit and a pleasure, once new eating patterns are established they can become an equally pleasurable new habit. Fig. 16 shows that it can be done.

Wives have a responsibility here. They tend to think that they have to demonstrate their skill and virtue by producing large meals when small ones will do. Husband does not like to disappoint and seem ungrateful, so he eats more than he needs or wants. Ladies, you are more likely to be a widow if you have a plump husband!

152

Third – Exercise. By this is meant reasonable physical activity so that you can run for a bus or go briskly upstairs without disgracing yourself.

Exercise, and it does not matter how you take it, physical jerks, weight lifting, walking, playing games, gardening, has a number of virtues. Not only does it keep the heart fit – remember the bus conductors – but it also blows away the cobwebs and makes you feel better. The important thing is that if possible you should choose a form of exercise that you really enjoy. It need not be competitive but it should be brisk. It is never too late to start being physically active, but if it is a long time since you did it might be wise both to consult your doctor and then get fit under supervision. Remember that as you get older what you have can be retained, what is lost is difficult to retrieve. The spry old folk are the ones who have been active all their lives. Fat goggle-box watchers tend not to make old bones.

Remember too that exercise, although it does use up a few Calories, is a relatively poor way of losing weight. The 19th hole and the rugby club bar may well put you into Calorie credit.

Walk upstairs, walk part of the way to work, get out at weekends and participate in group physical activity. Often we advise our patients to buy a dog and then it will take you out in the evenings.

Fourth – Do not smoke cigarettes. Pipes and cigars are allowed. Cigarette smokers are more likely to have:

 Coronary thrombosis
 Chronic bronchitis
 Lung cancer
 Raised cholesterol
 A horrid cough
 and nasty yellow fingers.

Cigarette smoking puts up blood pressure, may calm the nerves, costs a lot of money and is an addictive form of air pollution.

153

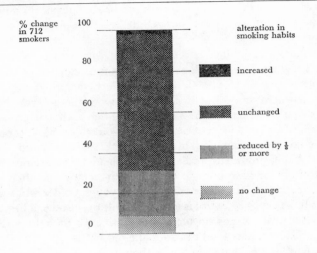

FIG. 17. Changes in smoking habits in 712 men a year or more after first examination. Note that it is possible to stop or reduce smoking. Source: Institute of Directors Medical Centre.

Even though one may have smoked for 40 years, it is still well worth stopping. Put the money you would have spent into a tin and have a second honeymoon. It is likely to be better than the first, now that you know what life is really about. Fig. 17 shows that success can be achieved.

Fifth – Alcohol. Alcohol is another common addiction, but it is also a desirable social lubricant and modest tranquillizer. One of its major disadvantages is that it is a high Calory food, and so if any quantity is taken appropriate debits must be set up in the Calory balance sheet.

We believe that alcohol in modest quantity is a thoroughly desirable component of modern living.

Sixth – Living with an understanding stress. Much has been said about this in the course of the book. Stress arises from failure or relative failure and is to a degree a measure of the individual's inability to recognize his own limitations. Getting fun out of life, and satisfaction out of what you do is one of the keys to survival.

If you have anxieties or stress symptoms, analyse them, identify them and then come to terms. The old adage says – a problem shared is a problem solved. Bring problems out into the open, discuss them freely, know your own devil and he will cease to bite you.

But remember that every man has his breaking point and the threshold for some is higher than for others. Most of us are born average. It is not given to many of us to succeed by breaking the rules. Few outstanding people are seriously stressed, they would never have got to the top if they were.

In the stress field there is a need to improve the quality of inter-personal relations, in the family, at work, in the unions and in politics. We cannot solve our problems by retreating into the make-believe world of pop and TV. We must actively participate.

Seventh – Regular health maintenance. Motor-cars and any piece of apparatus with moving parts, is better for both regular servicing and wise handling. The human body is part hydraulic pump and closed circuit water system, part telephone exchange and part heat engine. It responds to careful driving and periodic checks. Look after it well and it will keep you going for years. Abuse it and it will let you down.

Much disease is preventable and much can be picked up early before it has done real harm. Screening clinics are the thing of the future. Control of blood pressure and cholesterol is possible (Figs. 18 and 19).

Finally, one must sound a word of warning. In trying to be realistic about what happens to people one can only talk in terms of statistical probability. If one takes 100 fat cigarette

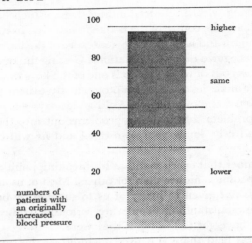

FIG. 18 (above). Change in blood pressure in 98 men who were found to have raised pressure at first examination; a year or more later. Source: Institute of Directors Medical Centre.

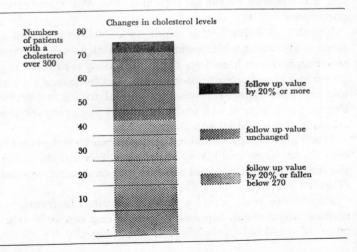

smokers, *this* is what is likely to happen to say 70 of them, or 100 women with breast cancer may behave in the same way. What we cannot at present say, with any certainty, is which 70 will go one way and which 30 the other. Thus a given individual may break the rules and survive, whereas another will observe all the virtues and succumb. Doctors cannot, in their limited wisdom, write a blank cheque or issue a passport to eternity. All we can do is to advise you as to how best the dice can be loaded in your favour.

FIG. 19 (left). Change in cholesterol level in 77 men who originally had a raised blood cholesterol at first examination, followed up for at least a year. Source: Institute of Directors Medical Centre.

Bibliography

Further recommended reading

Modern Weight Training, Al Murray, Kaye and Ward – for the specialist

Basic Weight Training, Al Murray, George Grose – for the beginner

5 BX plan for men and women, Royal Canadian Air Force, Penguin – free-standing exercises, no apparatus required.

Active Alerted Posture, Professor W. E. Tucker, E. & S. Livingstone

For the interested layman

Relaxation – a key to better living, J. Macdonald Wallace, Parrish

Physical fitness for busy men, I. J. MacQueen, M.B., F.R.C.S., Director Publications

Arthritis and Rheumatism, Dr. W. S. C. Copeman, Evans

This Slimming Business, Professor John Yudkin, Penguin

A New Look at Nutrition, Mary F. Crowley, Pitman

Coronary Case, Rex Edwards, Faber

Index